EYELASH
INDUSTRY IN
FRANCE **22-23**

BACK TO BASICS
EYEBROW SHAPING
50-51

BACK TO BASICS
– CUSTOMER
SERVICE **60**

CONTENT

WELCOME TO THIS ISSUE / 3

I0408850

WELCOME TO ISSUE 6 OF LASH INC

We have lots of interesting articles this issue, new contributors and new ideas.
This journal is for you the lash artist and we have expanded our reader gallery so we can showcase more of your work.
If you are interested in contributing to the magazine please contact info@lashinc.eu
Issue 7 will be released in July until then, have a great Spring season.

Louise Prunty

Louise Prunty
Editorial director / Business

Francine Widdows
How to attract customers

Michelle Ryan
Self Preservation

Melanie Doyle
Beauty Editor

Ruth Morrison
Eyebrow Shaping

Kim Gibb
Lash Bug Article

Britta Krueger
Let your passion take over

Richard Prunty
Editorial assistant

Enisa Becar
Designer

The views in the articles of Lash Inc are the views of individual contributors and do not necessarily reflect that of the company.

Lash Inc.
7 Newton Place, Lower Ground, Glasgow, G3 7PR

Contact Name: Louise Prunty
Contact Email: info@lashinc.eu
www.lashinc.eu

FLAWLESS L'LASHES
Loretta's Lash Academy & Beautique

www.eueyelashinstitute.com
info@eueyelashinstitute.com

Group Volume Training

7 Volume Techinques
★★★★★

by Loreta J
International Master Lash Artis

Our new super fast lash glue-recommendedfor experienced lash technicians only.

Sets in 1 second polymerizes in 1s Strong eyelash glue manufactured and specially formulated in compliance with EU regulations.

Ideal for both classic 1:1 and Russian volume eyelash extensions.

wwww.flawlesslashesproducts.co.uk

We ship worldwide !

admin@flawlesslashesproducts.co.uk

Lashes

THE METROSEXUAL

AN UNTAPPED MARKET FOR THE EYELASH EXTENSION INDUSTRY

Ask any woman and most will tell you that they find dark, full lashes on a man very attractive. The Metrosexual is a prospective market that is a potential goldmine.

The typical metrosexual is a young man with money to spend, living in or within easy reach of a metropolis — because that's where all the best shops, clubs, gyms and hairdressers are. He might be officially gay, straight or bisexual, but this is utterly immaterial because he has clearly taken himself as his own love object and pleasure as his sexual preference [1]

I have been doing lashes for almost five years and in that time I have only had one male client. He is one of my regulars. He has worn both real mink fur as well as synthetic faux mink. The lash extensions I choose are dependent on the look that he wants to achieve and on the condition of his natural eyelashes. Having long, full, eyelashes are a sign of youth and as we age, they become finer, thinner, and shorter. If a client wants a more youthful appearance then I suggest applying real mink fur extensions that are slightly longer than his natural eyelashes. This gives a natural thickness that is commonly associated with youth. If he wants a more noticeable mascara look then I suggest synthetic faux mink extensions. These give him a longer, thicker look that is more consistent with wearing mascara without the pitfalls that come with mascara.

However, if eyelash extensions aren't for your male client, there are products and services other than eyelash extensions that we can offer the Metrosexual. How about guyliner, manscara, and strip lashes? Lash lifts and heated eyelash curlers are also alternatives. Guyliner and manscara is eye make-up mar-

keted for men. As you have probably already guessed, guyliner is eyeliner for men and manscara is mascara for guys. Is there any difference between this and women's make up? Probably not, but it sounds cooler. Some companies that sell male eye cosmetics are guylinerTM and MYEGO. And what about strip lashes for the metrosexual? They come in discreet, natural looking styles marketed for men.

Eylure and HeadcoversTM Unlimited are companies that sell strip lashes geared specifically to the metrosexual.

For a man that wants to make his eyes more noticeable without the fuss that eye make-up can pose or the maintenance that eyelash extensions have, consider offering him a lash lift. This is a relatively new service that salons are adding to their menu. Unlike lash perms that curl the lashes downward at the tips and can make long lashes look shorter, a lash lift curls the natural lashes up at the base, making his eyelashes more noticeable and giving the eyes a more "awake" look.

Finally, a heated eyelash curler is something that we can offer the Metrosexual. This is a battery operated device that is specifically designed to gently curl the natural eyelashes without causing the damage that traditional manual eyelash curlers may do. By placing the natural lashes on the curler, then rolling and pressing the curler against the lashes, he can add curl and lift to his lashes in ten to fifteen seconds! Remember that this curl is tempo-rary and may need to be repeated throughout the day.

Metrosexuals take pride in their appearance and the eyelash extension industry should seriously consider paying more attention to them. After all, they have the disposable income to afford regular eyelash grooming and all of the aftercare products that go along with it. Isn't that the ideal client that we are all looking for?

By Lise Smith
Certified Master Eyelash Technician and owner of Lash Me Up

1. *Simpson, Mark (22 July 2002). "Meet the metrosexual". Salon, July 2002.*

INTRODUCING LASH INC
LASH ARTIST OF THE YEAR
2015 - CONTEST SPONSORS

SINFUL LASHES 6D VOLUME
CATEGORY SPONSOR

Luxury products at competitive prices. Featuring our Red Ruby Volume Adhesive. Quality, in-depth training located in Los Angeles. We also travel the US bringing our Classic and Volume training to you.

Sinful Lashes
Luxury Products and Quality Training.
Tel-1-818-970-7151
Email-Sinfullashes@gmail.com
www.sinfullashes.com

FLIRTIES 2D-4D
VOLUME CATEGORY SPONSOR

"We are dedicated to not only supplying highest quality products but also to providing an excellent service. With our accumulated experience we source, create and produce innovative products for the professional health and beauty industry in order to make your life easier. Our products enable you to an easier and more efficient treatment that is comfortable and enjoyable for the client at high margins for you.

With our team of fully qualified and accredited trainers we will help you get started whether its a new venture for you or an addition to your existing treatment. By offering an all in one package with training, starter kits, essentials and marketing material we can support you throughout and not only on the training day but in the years thereafter."

Flirties offer - *A wide range of eyelash extensions, eyebrow extension and beauty products.*
http://www.beautytrix.me/
0845 022 22 33

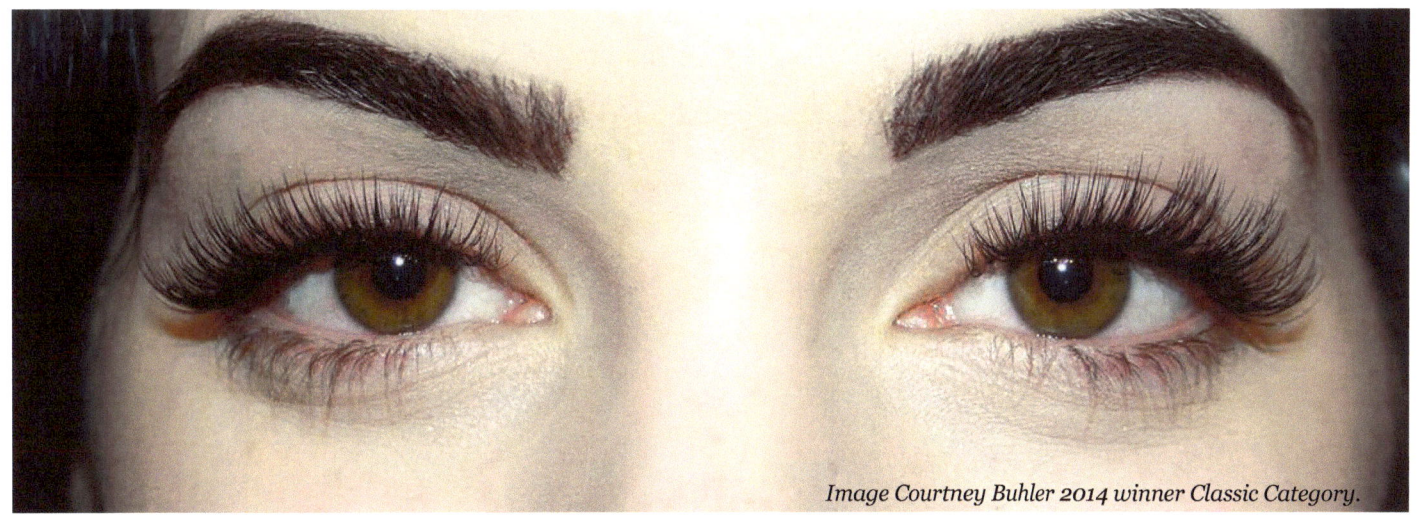

Image Courtney Buhler 2014 winner Classic Category.

LASH INC IRELAND
- CLASSIC CATEGORY SPONSOR

ttp://www.lashincproducts.com/

Lash Inc Ireland is the Lash Inc Journal with an expanded version featuring Irish ash artists, training providers and suppliers.

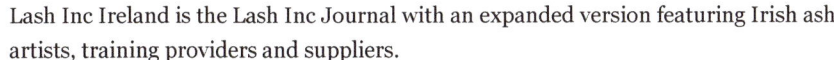

SUGAR LASH
LASH ART CATEGORY SPONSOR

SugarLash was created by Courtney Buhler (President + Founder of Lash Affair Inc). After years of great success in the lash industry, her passion for high-quality lashes has only grown stronger. *"Damaged lashes were something we were seeing all too much of in the lash industry, and I finally came to the conclusion that it wasn't necessarily the lash technicians fault. The level of training I would expect to find just wasn't available in our areas, so women were doing poor lashes, because of a poor education. This is where SugarLash came from. My passion is knowing my craft inside and out. This means not only doing beautiful lashes, but also understanding where lash extensions came from, what they are made out of, how adhesive works, sanitation for the eye area, eye anatomy & conditions, shaping for different eye shapes, mixing different lengths and curls within full sets and more. When you fully understand every aspect of your trade, success will easily follow. Client's want lash technicians that are passionate, knowledgeable, and confident - and those are the technicians SugarLash creates!* http://www.sugarlashpro.com | info@sweetsugarlashes.com | Tel: 1 (587) 982 -5274

Entries are now being accepted for Lash Artist of the Year - Contest 2015. Deadline is 14th Aug 2015.

Enter or enquires to email info@lashinc.eu
Join our group on Facebook: - Search ... Lash Artist of the year

Cost to enter £25 GBP or $40 USD
After you submit your photo you will be invoiced for payment and added to our judges group.

Entry criteria is available on the Lash Artist of the Year - Facebook group or on Lash Inc Magazine group.
Good Luck!

LET YOUR PASSION TAKE OVER!

Britta Krueger

The only way to do GREAT WORK is to love what you do.

We all have either experienced it ourselves or we know someone who grunts when the alarm goes off in the morning and it's time to get up and get ready for work (well most of us don't like getting up but hopefully many of you will be looking forward to going to work!).

If you don't enjoy what you do for a living then every hour of the day will stretch endlessly and a week seems an eternity!

Luckily the beauty industry has offered many of us the opportunity to turn our hobby and passion into a living. Some of us have become truly addicted to the service we provide, clients have become friends and days are not long enough for us to do what we like best!

It is utterly refreshing to see people enjoying themselves and seeing their job more like a hobby with so much passion, enthusiasm and

dedication to offer their clients the best possible treatment. It is very rewarding and fulfilling when clients come back happy and recommend you to their friends as one of the best and statements like "I would never go anywhere else" truly warm your heart. This is of course not even taking into consideration that some clients even bring you flowers, chocolates or even gifts as their sign of gratitude and appreciation for what you do for them.

Let's not forget.....it's not "just" treatments you offer! It is a time for a client to take a few minutes out of a busy schedule, time to relax, time for a chance, time to talk to someone else, someone they can share their burden or excitement of the day, time away from kids, housework or other chores. This is a truly special time for most clients who look forward to their regular treatments, not for the treatment procedure or outcome itself but for the whole experience it offers and sometimes we can even help with support and a shoulder for those who need it.

Being a therapist is fabulous if you enjoy it!

As years go by, therapists get more skilled, products and techniques evolve and some of us become a bit more adventurous and innovative. We owe those creative souls a huge

thank you for bringing new ideas and concepts to the industry and each treatment has got its own pioneers!

When a new idea is launched, there is quite a few people who will initially raise their eyebrows (hopefully nicely shaped :-) at the thought of something that might seem quite abstract but soon everyone warms to the new idea and people start asking to try this out.

The same happened when coloured lash extensions were first introduced. In the case they look bright and far too colourful, so regular clients were dubious and needing a bit of convincing to try them. Surprisingly once applied either with clear or black adhesive (for an even more subtle look) the different colours and the new options they offered to further enhance eye colour or other featured were endless and so began the advanced lash styling and lash art craze.

If you follow the trade press you would have seen some absolutely amazing transformations and skilful artistry for photo shoots and other events. Stunning models with fabulous and eccentric lashes to match the extraordinary make up are no rarity!
For the more subtle look those coloured lashes or two toned extensions (also called "ombre") can be applied in a way that the set can easily

be worn for everyday living or it can even be combined with some unique volumising techniques for a fuller look. For those of you who are unsure of volumising but want to create the fuller look, the new Ellipse lashes offer a perfect alternative and combined with glitter or pearlescent shimmer powders you can create an endless array of designs from classic, to accentuated or even dramatic!

All these ideas and designs could only evolve through passion and creativity of therapists who love working with lashes. In fact most of these lovely ladies actually dream and breathe lashes and it almost becomes an addiction, but a wonderful and fulfilling one!

Don't be shy, try something new, let your imagination and creativity run free and start experimenting with some ideas. If you feel unsure how to make a start it is definitely worth taking one of the advanced lash styling or lash art courses so that you can understand the basics of how to create the different looks and then you can start your own portfolio of amazing and stunning lash art transformation.

THE FIRST UK LASH CONVENTION

After being asked by so many of you we are excited to confirm the FIRST EVER UK LASH CONVENTION!

Date: Sunday 12th July 2015
Venue: Novotel London Heathrow airport.

Tickets are available from Eventbrite, simply search "Lash Convention 2015"
We are very happy to announce our special guest speakers:
Louise Prunty
Britta Krueger
Gina Mclaren
Hannah Putjato

This will be a golden opportunity to receive 4 mini-seminars by those highly regarded as some of the best in our business.

There will also be an opportunity to meet and mingle with fellow like-minded technicians & business owners, as well as view & purchase products from stalls.

This has been arranged for you at an exceptional introductory price of just £39.99!
Delegates are advised to book early to avoid disappointment, as spaces are limited!

Hosted by: Michelle Ryan and Francine Widdows.

PROFESSIONAL BEAUTY LONDON AND IRISH BEAUTY

The London show is one of the biggest events for UK beauty salons. People travel from all over the UK to see what new products are on offer. The show is large and their are many stands however if you are only looking for professional lash related items you will come across only a handful of suppliers.

Although Professional beauty London didn't have masses of eyelash companies attending, however the ones that did attend were of high quality and many with great offers on further training and products.

The 4 main lash brands attending were Nouveau Lash, Lash Perfect, My Beautiful Eyes and Lady Lash. All stands were very busy while many other surrounding stands were not so busy. Showing just how popular lashing is!

Nouveau Lash revealed their new branding and also their latest offer of free ultimate lash training with kits purchased. Their stand was one of the busiest with salons snapping up the offer. I managed to speak to the lovely Debbie Law a trainer who was performing a volume lash treatment on a client.

HD Brows offers a 7 step treatment for creating the perfect eyebrow. Lines of ladies queued to be booked in for the service on this luxurious looking stand.

Lash Perfect was busy offering a range of treatments, express lashes seemed to be the treatment of choice and Brow Perfect eyebrow extensions were the must try treatment. Eyebrow extensions are very on-trend in the UK at the moment.

My Beautiful Eyes were show casing their range of Mylash and Mybrows products. Mybrows is an eyebrow treatment creating a perfect shape and colour for your client. This was the treatment of choice at this stand.

Karen Betts Professional team demonstrated permanent make up. Permanent eyebrows are getting massively popular. Hair stroke brows look amazingly natural and defined.

Lady Lash stand had an array of products & her training courses available to book. Hannah (Lady Lash owner) was personally demonstrating on the stand. The rest of the Lady Lash team were dealing with a queue of people eager to purchase products.

The great thing about the show was the layout, Spa treatments had their own section as did professional beauty. A separate area was available for hair and retail. I would say the busiest stands at the shows were Nails, Lashes and Eyebrow suppliers. If your a lash artist who currently doesn't offer a brow service, I would seriously consider one.

IRISH BEAUTY

The Irish beauty show is one of my favourite trade shows. It has many brands that are not seen in the UK and there is always something new. Stands are mainly smaller than other trade show so it feels more friendly. Visitors are there to buy, and everywhere I looked money was being spent.

Highlights:

Ms Diva was offering demos on Russian volume and was inundated with books for their Cork and Dublin locations. Ms Diva also sold out of their new supersonic glue, which is ideal for Russian Volume.

Glamour lashes almost sold out of their entire lash stock. Their lash premier at the show was a hit, with buyer stocking up on quality supplies.

Lash Perfect were kept busy all day with treatments from eager visitors trying out Lash perfect and Brow Perfect treatments.

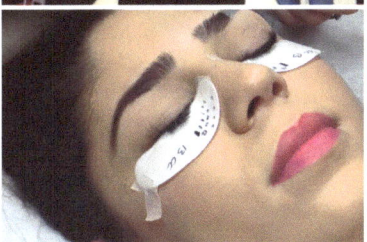

KEEPING UP-TO-DATE IN THE LASH INDUSTRY

Francesca Middleton

Embarking on a new career when it's a new profession, and especially when it's your own venture, is very exciting, challenging and a lot of damn hard work. But the rewards are many and the feelings of being a success are priceless.

With any new business venture putting together a business plan is essential, it is the foundation to your success and failing to do this will only restrict your ability to focus and build your business into a successful enterprise. Within your business plan it is vital to integrate your strategic plan on how to deliver, and to help with this you need to think about your training needs and how they will meet your business objectives. And as your business grows and develops it's important to realise that to meet these needs further training is essential. There are other areas that are important to plan but I'm going to concentrate on the training element here.

Once you've obtained the relevant skills to begin your business it is never good to be complacent and sit on your foundational training abilities. You will certainly naturally improve on your initial skill-sets, which is a testament to your dedication and drive to offer a quality service, but failure to continue with your training will mean that you will eventually plateau. Whilst others who do participate in further training will mean that you will be left behind as your competitors will move forward.

Being aware and using all the current technologies will get you to the top of your profession, but there are always new techniques being developed and it's important to stay on the ball and be aware of them. Of course depending on the subject matter there will come a time when there will be no more advancement however I am a trainer and I still find little nuggets of gold from fellow colleagues in my specialist field.

It is, of course, personal choice on how much to spend on training development and there are other calls to action that will help you be the best you can be which I have detailed below:

JOIN PROFESSIONAL FORUMS

It's a great way to connect with fellow colleagues who are just as passionate as you are in being a success in whatever field of profession you choose. It's a great way to get helpful hints and tips on how to improve skill-sets and trouble-shoot any problems that may arise. However it is no substitute for formal training as sometimes you need to be shown techniques and you need to be certified in professional skills.

EXPERIMENT WITH DIFFERENT BRANDS

The brand you trained with may not be the best one for you. Everyone is different and you may find similar products work better for you. I wouldn't recommend changing straight away though, I would give yourself at least 3 - 6 months with what you were given before experimenting. Your insurance will still be valid as the insurance companies are only interested in knowing that you have achieved a certain skill level with a certified training school.

SHADOW AN EXPERT OR FIND A MENTOR

A lot of learning is based on self-improvement and sometimes working on your own can make you feel like the blind leading the blind. Having the reassurance of someone guiding you whilst you're picking up your

skills or even watching an expert will help with your confidence that you are moving in the right direction.

CONTINUE WITH ADVANCED TRAINING

It's great to have a play around and discover new ways to improve your techniques. But using your paying clients might not be the best way to do this. Have a plan on when to move into formally improving what you already know. But don't rush into doing this, it's just as important to build up your confidence on what you already know before moving into new skill-sets. Only you will know when the time is right. Some professionals are naturally gifted and thus undertake further training faster than others or even feel the need not to. Use your own judgement on when the time is right for you.

USE YOUR TRAINING PROVIDER HELP SERVICE

Your training provider has a wealth of knowledge and experience and should be only too happy to help you get up to speed with your skill-sets and to help improve what you already know. Their reputation is based on their student's quality of skill-sets and they will want you to be their shining ambassadors.

KEEP UP-TO-DATE WITH MARKET TRENDS

It's important to be aware of how the business market develops and evolves. This is not to say that new trends will be better with your chosen field but it's important to have a knowledge and understanding of the concepts, benefits and disadvantages. Being able to advise your client-base on what treatments are best for them is a good way to be seen as an innovative professional looking after their needs.

CREATE A PROFESSIONAL RECOMMENDATION CIRCLE

Believe it or not, there will be times when you cannot see your valued clients. There will be times that you may be unable to work or perhaps enjoy an extended vacation. Don't let them fall prey to receiving a treatment that they could be disappointed with. As much as you value your business and skills, not everyone is quite so intent on providing excellence. Look after your clients and build up a network of fellow professionals in your area who you can recommend during your absences. They will do the same for you!

Remember - if you love what you do, you WILL be a success!
© LASH by Francesca – LASHacademy

LASH & BROW

Reader Gallery

Beauty Lashes by Katre

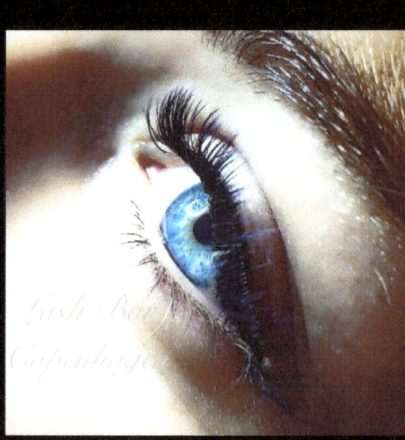

SINFULLASHES.COM

SINFULLASHES.COM

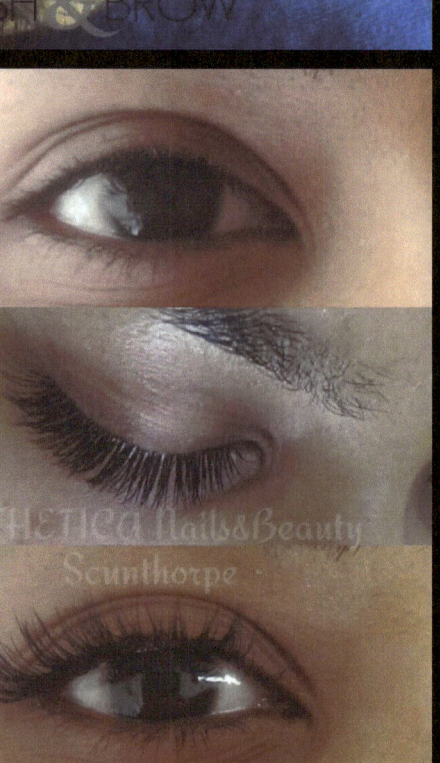

ESTHETICA Nails&Beauty Scunthorpe

Lash Factor

Rebekah Toffolon Matthews

Lash Envy MK

DorinaDor Cils, TOULOUSE

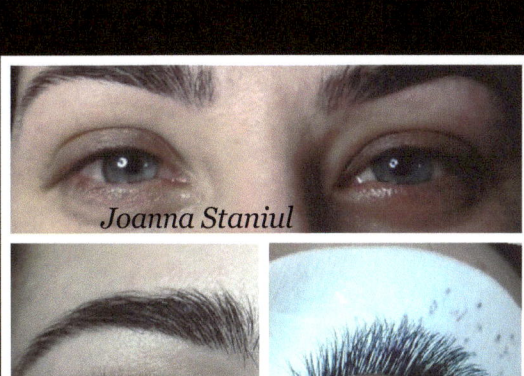

Joanna Staniul

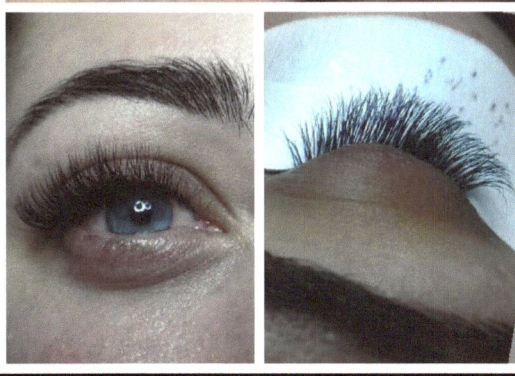

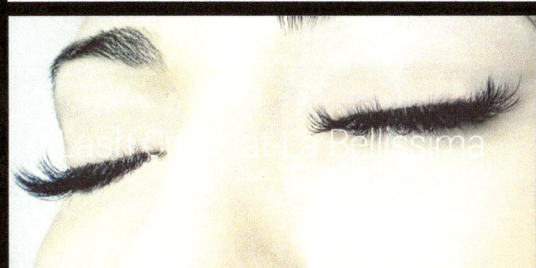

Lash Crush at La Bellissima

Lash Crush at La Bellissima

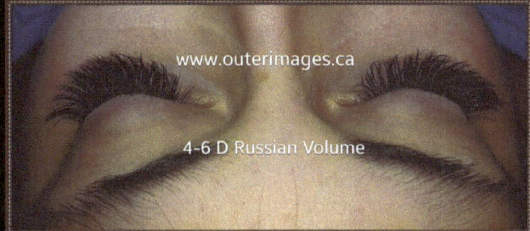

www.outerimages.ca

4-6 D Russian Volume

Leah Lynch

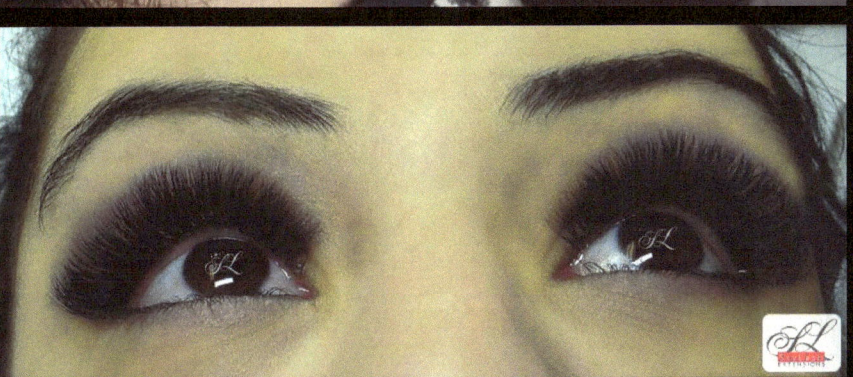

Gera-Király Anita

Lash Gabriel

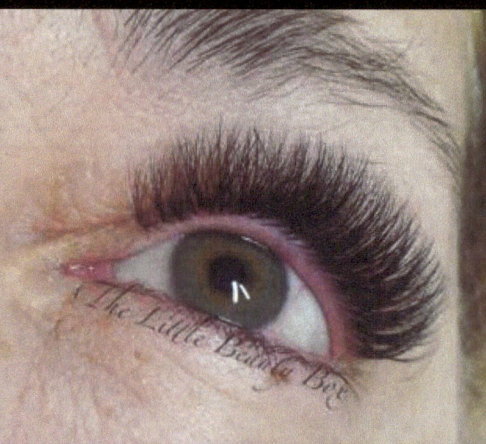

The Little Beauty Bee

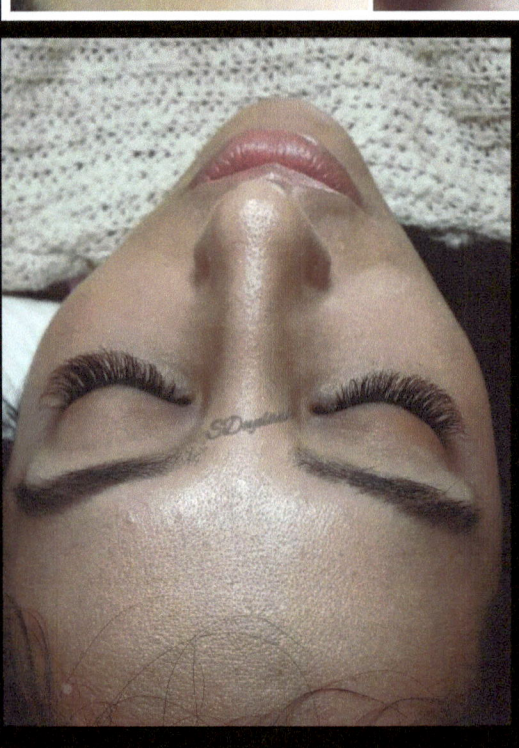

before

after

iLashtique

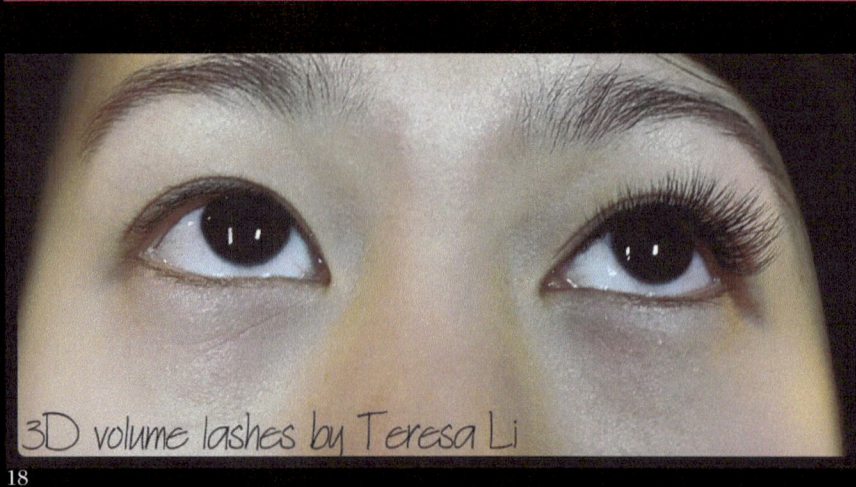

3D volume lashes by Teresa Li

@lash4lash

Sandra Karlsson

Claudia's Nail Design - Lashes

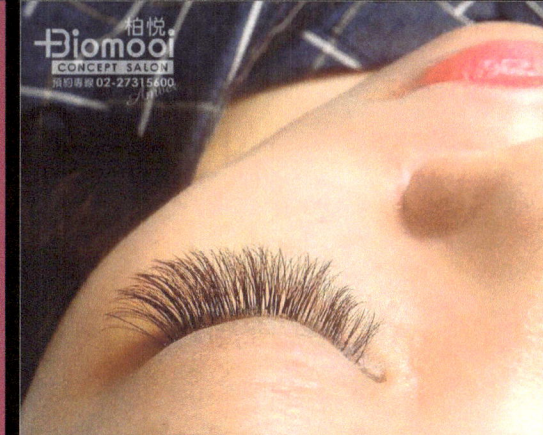

CLARITA SMIT
MAKE-UP, HAIR & LASH EXTENSIONS

Anne Bowcock

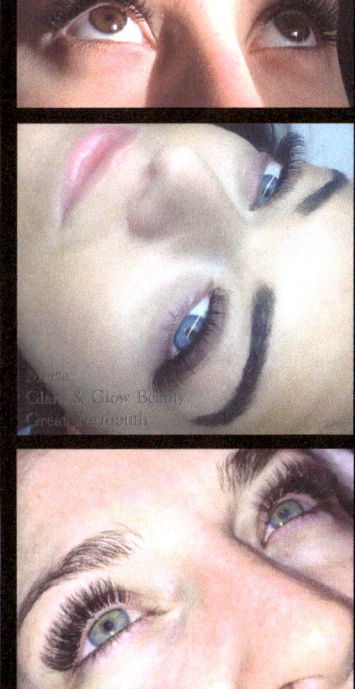

Leslie Kroeker

Sarah Humphreyson

Leanne Harber

Lash Art by Lesley @ Luscious Lashes Intl.

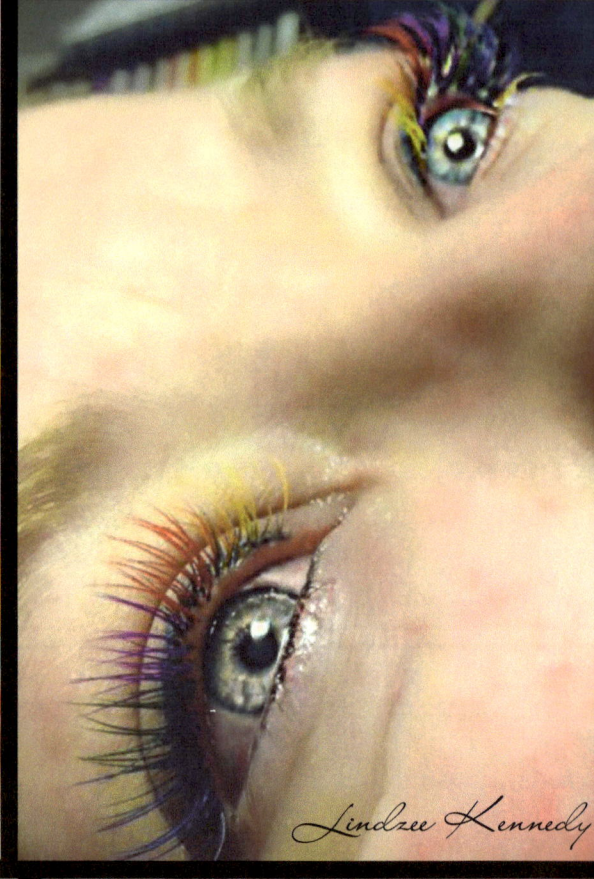

Lindzee Kennedy

Leanne Harber

Magdalena Mróz

Manami Edwards

Vicushka Lashes

Yolanda Odom

Sylvia Liu

Body Chic Boutique

Sarah Humphreyson

Timea Owsley

Tanja Nicklaus

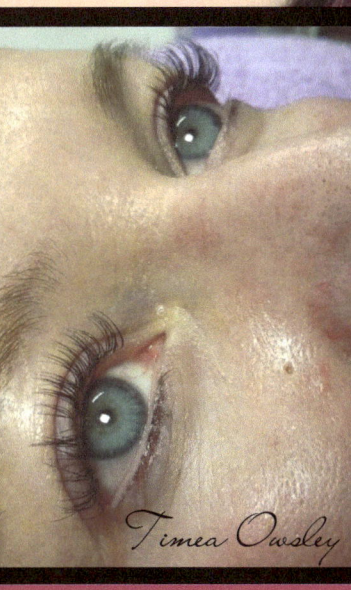
Timea Owsley

EYELASH INDUSTRY IN FRANCE

Bivol Dorina

Today, all of us know about eyelash Extensions, it's a practice that enhances the length, thickness and fullness to natural eyelashes. But not everyone knows yet, that the lash applying is an art.

In France, the first eyelash extension appeared in October, 2006. And even though almost nine years have been passed, the technique of eyelash extension remained at the same level in most of the beauty salons. Unfortunately you can still see classic eyelash extension done with 0.2 mm, even in luxury salons.

The main thing in this story, from my point of view, is that a large amount of esthetic centers from France still propose for theirs students, eyelash extension courses using lashes of 0.2 mm. This is why, a big number of eyelash artists from France, are going abroad for a new qualification.

In 2014 the new technique of eyelash extensions, volume extension, or "Russian Effect" as it is also called, was brought in France for the first time. This type of extension isn't still very popular in France, but slowly more and more women discover the biggest innovation to the lash world. I am quiet sure that all lashmakers, especially those who are in this sphere for a long time, will change their point of view, when they compare the quality of the new and old generation of lashes, making the right decision.

The biggest cities in France where you can have your eyelashes done are Paris, Lyon, Marseille, Strasbourg, Lille, Nice, Albi, Toulouse and Bordeaux. Usually the price of eyelash extensions varies between 99 € and 200 €, it depends on which kind of extension you want and which salon are you choosing.

Today, it isn't necessary to be a celebrity to attend an eyelash extension. Women from all around the world are catching on and becoming Lash Addicted!

SELF PRESERVATION

Michelle Ryan

One of the things I hear myself saying repeatedly to my friends, clients and fellow lash technicians is "being selfish is the most selfless thing you can be"

Basically, if you don't look after yourself, you can't be a rock for everyone else.

On our bad days we put on our smiley persona to greet our clients and when they come into our salons with the weight of the world on their shoulders, it is our duty to ensure they leave feeling refreshed, happy and ready to take on the world.
Even if they have the most beautiful lashes applied, unless that client leaves with a spring in their step we feel we haven't done our job properly and usually take it personally.

We spend hours in a seated position hunched over our clients, and I don't know about you but I know it's been a good day when my hand becomes "the claw" and looking up is like discovering a whole new world (once I regain focus!)

Despite the fact we constantly have clients coming in and out of our salons, it can be a very lonely profession.
It is our responsibility to ensure that our work isn't detrimental to our health, so here are a few things that will help you to stay focused, fresh and ready!

Something I have noticed about lash technicians is that we are perfectionists. Our standards are very high and we are hugely self critical.
Perfectionism is a major source of avoidable stress. You need to set reasonable standards for yourself otherwise you are setting yourself up for failure.

Learn to say "NO". Why do those two letters escape our vocabulary so often? Embrace them and realise by using them more often we give our self more time and less worry...go on, try it!
Being more assertive will help you in all areas of your life.

It's really important to surround yourself with positive people who will pick you up and enhance you, rather than bring you down.

Avoid people who stress you out. We will always meet people who we don't click with and that's ok, pass them on to someone who will appreciate them. You won't be able to give them your best service and they won't enjoy their treatment so it's not productive for you to keep them.

Try to view situations from a positive perspective.
"What you give out to the world comes back to you".
It is so true, and on my darkest days I smile harder!!
Look for ways that you can learn from the situation or what you can change so it doesn't happen again. Reflect on your strengths and look at how far you have come already.

Time management. This is an article in itself!
Making time for yourself is a priority! You need to set aside some time to switch off and relax.
I once saw a quote that said "meditate for 20 minutes every day. if you haven't got time, then you must meditate for an hour a day!" (source unknown)

Go for a walk
Watch a comedy
Have a good workout (a suggestion is pilates. It's great for core strength so will help to support our poor backs)
A long bath with candles
Fuss a pet
Get a massage
Read a book
Potter in your garden

It is really important to do something you enjoy every day and equally you need to keep your sense of humour. Laughter is a cure for almost everything!
As well as looking after our psychological wellbeing, we can also increase our resistance to stress and illness by looking after our physical health.
Exercise at least 30 mins a day, 3 times a week.
Eat a healthy diet. Make sure you have balanced, nutritious meals and don't skip breakfast!
Drink plenty of water.
Reduce your intake of caffeine and sugar. It produces temporary highs which result in a sudden drop in energy.
Avoid alcohol, smoking and drugs.
Make sure you get enough sleep.
Practice relaxation techniques.
But then you knew this already...

Most of the suggestions I have made can be incorporated into your working day. Prioritise your schedule and look where you can make small changes.

If you tend to finish work late and then start checking emails, researching product, practicing techniques, checking online forums etc.. then you need to take a step back.

Plan specific time when you will allow yourself to do these things and then add a time limit. This is still work, so you must plan it into your work schedule, otherwise you will always feel there isn't enough hours in the day.

Make sure anything work related is off and out of reach by a certain time, allowing yourself to do something completely relaxing before you go to bed.

Once you start incorporating these small changes they will become habit.
Lashing isn't just our job, it's a passion that we should enjoy!
"Don't be so busy treading water that you forget how much fun it is to swim"

EYELASH EXTENSIONS BREAKING THROUGH IN THE NETHERLANDS

In Eastern-Europe, the United States and in the United Kingdom the beauty scene cannot be imagined without eyelash extensions. This trend has definitely started to find its way to the Netherlands. Someone who anticipated this is Yvonne van Wieren, CEO and founder of Lash eXtend. Since 2010 she's a distributor of eyelash extensions, related products and supplies.

Beauty and personal care are second nature to me

"I have been interested in beauty and personal care since childhood. Shiny hair, beautiful skin and an attractive appearance are important to me. Being of Indonesian origin my natural eyelashes are short and straight. Six years ago I met somebody wearing eyelash extensions and I knew right away: 'That is what I want!'"

"From that moment on I have been looking into the eyelash extensions phenomenon. I followed courses in the Netherlands as well as other countries and started to practice applying eyelash extensions, testing many different products and techniques along the way."

"It didn't take long before I knew that this was going to be my new job. I saw a big opportunity because the market in the Netherlands still had to be developed. While doing my job as a personal assistant, I wrote a business plan for my own company and started preparing the launch of my own eyelash extensions business. I was ready to share my knowledge and experience with the rest of the Netherlands."

In 2010 Lash eXtend started its operation and has been online since 2013, Lash eXtend is the supplier of everything that is needed to apply eyelash extensions to give the eye more volume or to lengthen the natural eyelashes. What once started out as a part-time job soon turned into a full-time job because by now, hundreds of beauty salons are working with our brand.

On a daily basis many orders are being processed and parcels are being sent to the Netherlands, Belgium and Luxemburg. Demand for good quality products is steadily rising ever since.

Yvonne van Wieren
CEO & Founder Lash eXtend

In our own salon in Amersfoort we share our experience with other specialists by providing several training and education programs. We also have our own eyelash extension customers who leave the salon with a beautiful glance. Our youngest salon customer is aged 15 and the oldest customer is 69 years old. Beauty does not have an age restriction.

The Team

Lash eXtend currently consists of a team of 11 people, some of them the talents we discovered while giving training. All eyelash artists received further in-house training after which they joined the team. We all love and share the same passion for eyelash extensions and regularly meet to exchange the latest trends and beauty news.

Training

Every week we provide different training sessions to beauty specialists who would like to start using Lash eXtend products in their own salons. Before these specialists start using Lash eXtend products, we want to make sure they know everything necessary to be able to start working with the products.

The Lash eXtend team can also be found at various national and international beauty trade fairs. By participating at these fairs we are able to present Lash eXtend products to a much bigger audience and show off the latest techniques and eyelash trends.

Russian Volume Lashes

In order to stay up to date with the latest beauty trends our lash specialists also take courses in the Netherlands and abroad. We were trained by important names in the business like Loreta J, Irine Levchink and Nouveau Lashes. Recently we were able to bring the Russian Volume Lashes to the Netherlands. 3D already existed here, but we have added our own Lash eXtend flavour to this, resulting in stunning results.

Masterclasses

Delivering quality products and training has top priority for Lash eXtend. That is why we have introduced several master classes enabling eyelash artists to become the best in what they do. Also for the Russian Volume technique we offer a master class. During this master class we teach trainees to create even more volume using 4-6 different techniques.

These master classes are only suitable for experienced eyelash stylists who already mastered the regular techniques like classic lashes and express lashes.

Eyelash trends in the Netherlands

In the Netherlands we are still lagging behind when compared with other countries like the United Kingdom. We have always been a bit conservative in comparison with the trendsetting countries and the experts are mainly coming from the USA, the UK and several Eastern European countries. The news outlets in those countries pay more attention to eyelash trends, which is why most trends and new knowledge comes from abroad. This does not mean however that there is no talent in the Netherlands.

More and more women are aware of their lashes and this is notable by the huge increase in demand for Lash eXtend products. My goal is to further expand into the European market. It took me 2 years to change from a personal assistant to successful entrepreneur. I love my job, I love the beauty business and I hope I can share my knowledge and experience for a long time to come!

OUT WITH THE OLD *IN WITH THE NOUVEAU*

NOUVEAU LASHES, THE AWARD-WINNING BRAND THAT PIONEERED THE MOST SIGNIFICANT LASH TREATMENTS IN THE BEAUTY INDUSTRY TODAY – INCLUDING STATE-OF-THE ART INDIVIDUAL EXTENSIONS AND THE REVOLUTIONARY LVL NATURAL LASH TREATMENT – IS SET TO SHAKE-UP THE LASH WORLD YET AGAIN, WITH A BRAND NEW LOOK, FEEL AND A REVOLUTIONISED APPROACH TO PROFESSIONAL TRAINING.

Extensive research carried out by Nouveau Lashes has discovered that when it comes to lashes, every woman's looking for something different; one client's version of the 'dream lash' varies significantly from the next, varying between a completely natural look to a high-octane glamorous result. Therefore, as lashes holds its position as one of the industry's fastest growing beauty essentials, offering just one treatment is simply no longer enough.

Introducing Nouveau Lashes' Ultimate Technician Programme, where beauty professionals can master the entire extensive portfolio of the brand's exclusive treatments in a single package – covering 'Extend', classic Nouveau Lashes extensions, 'Express', formally Let's Go strip, individual extensions and lash fillers, and 'LVL Enhance', the brand's famous semi-permanent natural lash lengthening, volumising and lifting treatment. The Ultimate Technician Programme means, for the first time, technicians can cater for every client's desires and unlock new success in their business.

The Ultimate Technician Programme is divided into two comprehensive courses - split to allow technicians to refine their technique, and immediately enjoy the financial benefits of their new skills during the course of their training, whilst eliminating the unnecessary cost & hassle of training in multiple single treatments.

What's more, Nouveau Lashes has experienced a complete new rebrand. As three become one, with the Ultimate Technician Programme, the fresh premium colour palette, new world-class brand photography and polished design will feature across all treatment and product ranges, in-salon marketing materials and the newly launched advice and information-packed website*. This new look and feel for Nouveau Lashes is designed to emphasise the brand's ultimate lash brand status

and allow salons to maximise the benefits of offering superior Nouveau Lashes treatments with a brand their clients will trust and ask for by name.

Karen Betts, lash pioneer and Nouveau Lashes co-founder says: *"We have reached a point where it's no longer viable for lash technicians to train individually in different lash disciplines - it's limiting for their business and more costly for them. Ask any lash technician and they will tell you that lashes are not a passing trend, it is, in fact, a beauty essential - and clients increasingly want more choice and better results, which is just so exciting for our industry.*

"By training in all areas of Nouveau Lashes, extend, express and LVL enhance, over two short courses, equating to just five days in total, technicians will save time, money and, ultimately, enjoy healthier profits – and fast!"

Industry innovator and Nouveau Lashes co-founder Bridgette Softley adds: *"This new, elite approach to training was born out of us really listening to salons and technicians The traditional approach to training wasn't working for them. Our simplified Ultimate Technician training eliminates overlap and confusion, allowing for maximum focus on technical skill, commercial training and the all-important client consultation.*

"Fully understanding the evolving needs and desires of the consumer market is the lifeblood of Nouveau Lashes. Our consumer insight and knowledge enables us to provide the exact solutions and training needed to enable technicians to satisfy the growing hunger for great lashes and grow their business".

MY LASH REVELATION

It was love at first sight for me when I saw my first set of eyelash extensions. Those gorgeous green eyes. I couldn't stop staring. She looked years younger than the last time I'd seen her and it seemed like her eyes were literally smiling at me. From that moment on I was hooked. I knew I had to learn how to do eyelash extensions.

It seemed so simple when I first heard the idea. Glue one extension to one eyelash. I looked at pictures online of incredible lash artistry and thought I'd be able to do the same thing. I was so ignorant as to the amount of work it would be beginning my new career. Thank heavens I'm a totally neurotic perfectionist that doesn't know the meaning of quit. After certifying and doing lots of new sets and fills I had grown more confident. Maybe too confident that I knew what I was doing and could give anyone a beautiful set of lashes. I'd studied lash styles, application techniques, face and eye shapes. I'd practiced hour after hour and had built a steady client base. I was loving doing eyelash extensions full time.

One day I had a client walk through my door wanting lash extensions. Nothing in that request was new. She told me she'd been to 5 other lash artists and was told it was impossible. I felt my stomach in my throat as I looked at her lashes. I can't remember there being a straight undamaged lash on either eye. While there weren't any true holes in her lash line her lashes were thin, sparse and curly. Some were even growing completely curled around her lash line into the eyeball. I didn't want to be another lash artist sending her on her way and at the same time I knew I was about to embark on the biggest challenge of my career to date. We had a long discussion and I was worried because her lashes looked so fragile. My fear was causing damage and leaving her with even less options in the future. I did a set of .12 diameter lashes. I knew they didn't give her the look she wanted, but I also knew I hadn't damaged her lashes any further. I could only place about 40 extensions an eye and it took 2 hours. I charged her as a partial set knowing I'd done my best and it wasn't

good enough. I never saw her again. She changed my career. I learned I didn't know as much as I thought I did and I wanted to be better. Much better.

I was completely humbled realizing that the hours of practice I had done thus far was so inadequate when I was faced with doing her lashes. It was at that moment that the reality if I was ever going to truly be a master lash artist I would have to practice and work harder than I ever imagined. Just like a concert pianist practices scales, finger placement and touch on the keys, I would have to dedicate myself to the process of acquiring the skills and techniques needed in lashing.

She set me on a path to not just being a lash artist but inspired a dedication to becoming a true specialist of the craft. I am still in the process of becoming in this field. As a student initially certifying in lash extensions I learned techniques and end results. I learned a few basic ways to practice but not the kind of techniques needed to handle the problems. I discovered I had to learn how to practice effectively. Practice makes perfect. However if I practice imperfectly I get a perfectly imperfect result. I had to discover and develop new ways that worked for me to truly hone my skills. I practiced and still regularly practice many different techniques.

I sit on or tape up a set of practice lashes to distort them before placing them on my mannequin. I can then work with lashes that were going all different directions and misshapen. I replicate curly lashes by using practice lashes and tweezers to hold a section of lashes or an individual lash while twisting and turning the lashes to create new shapes. I set the changes using a gentle heat source then rapidly cooling.

I also had to learn new extension application techniques. One is to isolate a lash needing correction and hold it by the tip to straighten the twist or curl. While still holding the lash I swipe its entire length with a small amount of glue using the extension. Bond the extension

to the base holding it the direction the extension should go with tweezers. Then wrap the natural lash around the extension using the curl to my advantage. Since the natural lash is coated with glue using this technique, the extension weight may need to be adjusted so I don't create too much stress on the natural lash. Extensions applied this way will always be stiffer and weigh more due to the coating of glue. It is also really important to be sure I keep minimal pressure on the lash I'm holding. I've learned to watch the lash line and if the skin moves, or the practice lash lifts from the mannequin head, I am using too much pressure. It should feel soft in my hands and on the clients lashes. The lash line and the natural lash should never distort due to pulling.

Other correction techniques are attaching the extension at the base only in it's correct position while allowing the natural lash to go wherever it's going to go on it's own. Extensions can be applied on top of, to either side or behind the natural lash. I try to be creative in placement.

I have also used heated lash curlers to straighten lashes. I use the curler to create a change in the direction of the curl or sometimes just to soften the natural curl of the lashes. I can even lift a downward facing eyelash to a new lifted position. I can use the tip or the whole wand depending on what correction needs to be made to the lashes. This only works before applying a new set. I avoid putting heat on any extended lashes.

I have spent hours practicing techniques this way. Creating the problem in practice lashes has taught me more about how they develop in my clients lashes. It has also dramatically improved my isolation and application with lashes not requiring correction.

Last May when a customer found her way to my salon we began an incredible journey that continues to this day. Due to my prior preparation my stomach was no longer in my throat. Instead, I was excited because I knew I was prepared and could give her a stunning set of extensions.

I documented the starting lashes with photos so I could see at each appointment what had changed in her natural lashes. It allowed me to really closely watch for any signs of damage. This is what my clients lashes looked like in May 2014.

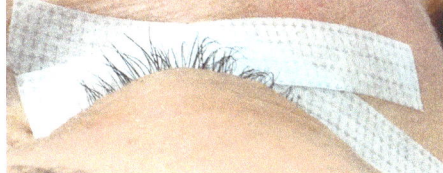

The first step was to do a thorough consultation. I had to identify why the lashes were in their present condition. In this case she slept on her side and moved a lot in her sleep. It caused rubbing and twisting on her natural lash. We discussed the problem and solved it by creating barriers to sleeping on her lashes. Placing a hand under her cheek to prop up her lashes off the pillow, pillow cases that have a slick texture and a sleep mask made to create a space that protects eyelash extensions. She agreed to do all of those things. Then we focussed on what she wanted from the extensions. I asked what she hoped to see when she looked at her new lashes in the mirror? She wanted to feel feminine and draw attention to her eyes. She had always felt that her lashes were nonexistent. She simply wanted to see them and be able to emphasize

her eyes. She'd never had long lashes and length was more important to her than volume. At this point we both understood the goals and I explained that I would do everything I could to provide a beautiful set of extensions that kept her natural lashes as healthy as possible.

When I approach extending this type of eyelashes I systematically extend the easiest lashes first. It becomes easier to isolate as I go along in the process. I usually leave the ones requiring the most work until the end or at least until the point where isolation can easily be achieved. This allows me to see the overall look and in some cases it's possible to leave some lashes unextended without compromising the appearance. However when that isn't possible, as in this case, it becomes necessary to employ the skills and tricks acquired during my practice sessions.

What I have learned is that when it comes to working with lashes that are out of the ordinary there are few rules. The first and most important one is to cause no harm.

As an artist I have to know my strengths and weaknesses. I always go to what I know. If I'm doing something new it's on practice lashes or a friend who knows I'm practicing something new. I never try something new on a paying client first. I stick to what I know and learn what skills I need to develop in practice.

I have to know the difference between a weak damaged lash and what is simply not an ordinarily shaped lash. From that base I can create a plan of action with my client.

When you combine a client that will take care of their lashes and adjust environmental factors that caused damage with a lash artist that utilizes correct extension weight and application techniques you create a powerful partnership. It is very possible to see dramatic positive changes even while wearing eyelash extensions. I removed my client's lashes to give her a new lighter fluffier set of extensions in February 2015. We went from a .18 diameter silk lash to a mix of .15 & .10 (capped with .07) diameter silk lashes. I was so happy to

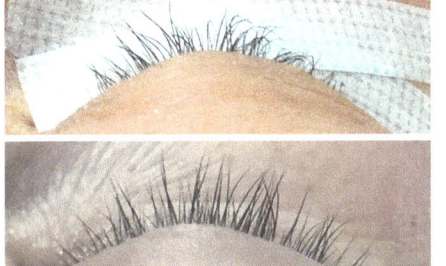

see the improvement in not just the direction of growth but also the overall strength of the natural lash.

Top Image: client lashes prior to having initial set of extensions May 2014
Bottom Image: client lashes after removal of lashes worn continuously since May 2014 and prior to new set in February 2015

It is so helpful to nurture within ourselves an attitude of curiosity and desire to improve. If something doesn't work for you try something different. It's okay to not know how to do something. Although nothing can replace a great mentor, don't feel like you have to wait for someone else to teach you. Be fearless in trying new things. Just do it using wisdom in your approach. Work it out, develop a pioneering attitude and don't be afraid to create something new. That's how this industry grows. Let the unknown propel you to creating a new known. Then practice, practice and practice even more. It's worth practicing. After you figure it out remain willing to share it with another lash artist. We all get better with an attitude of generosity when it comes to knowledge and skills.

I found that if I work hard to elevate my techniques and skills, use good judgement and honestly communicate with my client we can plot an effective course to get them to their ultimate desired look. Anything is possible.

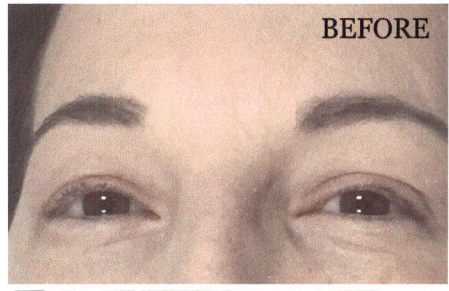

Top 2 images are from May 2014, .18 silk lashes. Bottom 2 images are from February 2015 .15 & .10 (capped with .07) silk lashes

Lisa Magee
Owner Lash Riot, Denver, CO

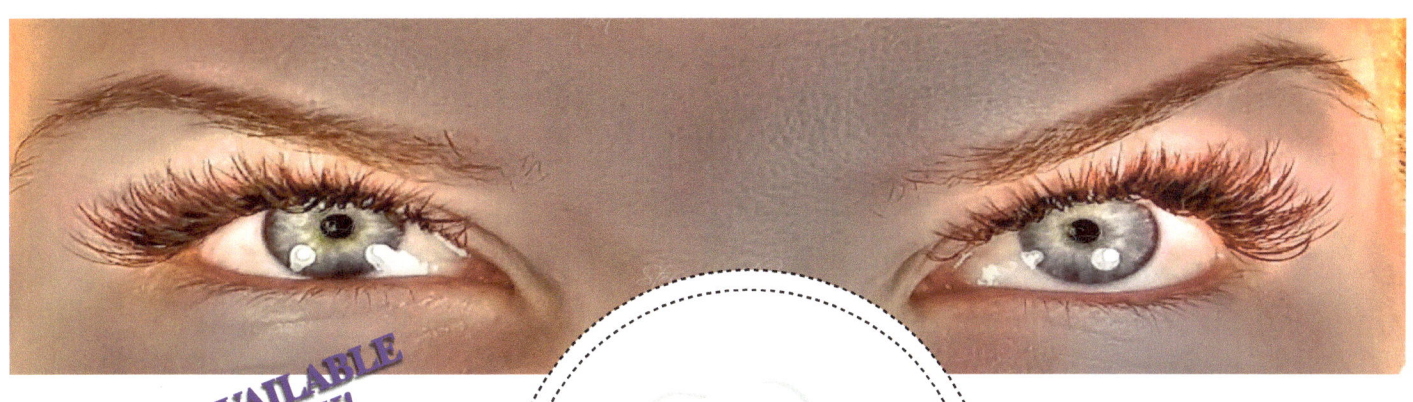

Skyn lash
ACADEMY

New Jersey's First & Only Lash School

Stefani Altieri,

Certified Master Lash Educator & Licensed Medical Esthetician

Co-Author Of Lash Masters Bookjudge & Sponsor Of Lash Wars 2014

Passionate About Lash Education & Has Traveled Around The World For

The Best Of The Best Training Certified From 7 Different International Well Known Lash Educators

As Well As BALAA (Be An Amazing Lash Artist & Lash Mastery Group In Beauty Industry 14+Yrs Lashing 9+Yrs

Always researching for the best of the best products & 1 step ahead of the latest trends
working hard to bring you the most efficient way of working giving you all the little details that most won't
tell you to make your job easier. (tips n' tricks)

Proud Member of NEESA   Certified & Proctor of ADFEE

NEW ONLINE INTENSIVE VOLUME *Early 2015*
lash training & mentoring program

lash training programs by Stefani Altieri

Basic Beginner Classic OR Volume Level 1 3/4/5/7 Day
Volume Technique Level 2 - 2 or 3 Day
Volume Advanced Refresher - 1 Day
Design Artistry - 1 Day & much more
Train The Lash Trainer - Become A Certified Lash Trainer
Train The Lash Educator - Already Certified Trainers Online

www.skynlashacademy.com
all new website   formerly www.skinlashstudio.com

ASKING THE QUESTIONS

Bobbi April

Cruelty Free Siberian Mink... Right? WRONG! But is it just the lashes... what about what goes down with the testing of "Medical grade adhesives"

Real fur (Mink, Fox, Squirrel now?) for Eyelash Extensions, we hear it all the time. But, have you actually stopped to think how it gets from the animal to you? Or in the case of adhesives... what happened to the animal in testing that could happen to you? Ironic... karma maybe?

Ever since I started my lash journey in 2010, I've known that real mink is a big no no. How do I know? Firstly, people will say whatever they want (or heard) swiftly and thoughtlessly to make money vs the reality of what actually goes down.

Reality.

Over the past 4 year's, I've spoken to many Lash Technicians and Supplier's regarding real fur lashes. Some people are aware and would never knowingly buy real fur, other's don't even stop to think and maybe they don't care, and then there's the ones who believe there are humane farms that brush the animal's, yet they will never actually show this proof. The fact is that ALL OF US are supporting the trade of fur, how? Because our main supplier's are buying it from fur farms and making it into eyelash extensions. Whether or not we buy fur is irrelevant, we are buying from manufacturers and factories that buy fur.

In the past year I've spoken to numerous manufacturers in Korea and also one of the main Eyelash Extension supplier's in Los Angeles who also sell on Ebay, on several occasions about what they are told about where the fur comes from and I'm given the very short answer "It's humane" But how?

When I ask the manufacturers in Korea, China, Vietnam or Japan about where they get the fur, it's quite easy to dismiss the question with the language barrier.

Sorry if you were under the dreamy assumption that the fur industry has lovely, big green pastures with thousands of kind

and gentle people brushing WILD animal's. No, they don't collect fur at a Zoo for Eyelash Extensions and come on now... it's still a ZOO if they did! but they don't. See, what actually

goes down is a really disturbing thing called Fur Farming.

Fur farming is where thousands upon thousands of wild foxes, minks and other beautiful innocent animals are being held in tiny boxes and bred purely for their coats. No living, breathing creature should ever be made

to endure this treatment... and for beauty? Do we not see how disgusting that is? No, because we're NOT in there seeing it.

Wild Mink's and other animal's like foxes normally roam kilometers of "Natural" habitat, not circling a tiny, grated, bottomless box. This stressful environment can lead to cannibalism and so they are then boxed alone where they are prone to self mutilation. Call it self mutilation or call it suicide, I know what I'd be contemplating. Once the animal's die, their carcasses are ground up and fed to the remaining animals and in some cases, the coats are torn from the dying animal's. It hurts to even say that but I've seen footage where people have gone in to expose what really goes down. All you have to do is google fur farming.

Now to "Medical Grade" adhesives and animal testing. That's right, those medical grade adhesives we all wanted because of the revelation that Cyanoacrylate polymerization produces Formaldehyde, and often contains other really harmful chemicals... well Medical Grade adhesives are adhesives that were originally used for wound closure. How did they find out that they can be used on humans? Off course scientists don't use humans, they use rabbits. So let's also ask the question, "How is this adhesive actually Medical Grade?".

We've all heard of "Crazy glue" or Super glue. Have you ever stopped to think what the difference is? Different branding, manufacturers, uses, the different chemical levels. Is it really that different?

Personally, I've been coming to a point where I feel helpless in the search to find concrete evidence that we have a "100% damage free" or cruelty free way of performing this treatment (For myself and my Client's), Yet we chat on these facebook groups, giving our opinions on different lash diameters and way's of cleansing and if we don't do it that way then we're not as professional or safe as that person. I don't know where to turn to to purchase products

without supporting something that doesn't sit right with me on a moral level.

This is all without even touching on the politics of the industry between trainer's, new up and coming supplier's and all us followers who want to be buying from that top notch company or be seen to be in with "The flavor of the month". Shouldn't it be about supporting those businesses that are doing all they can to elevate our industry, passionately and ethically?

When I was given the opportunity to do a write up for Lash Inc. magazine about real fur lashes, Initially I thought, how wonderful. The thing is, I've tried to create awareness about this and many other factors of our industry from the very start of my career, It wasn't winning me any friends and I'm pretty sure this isn't either, but winning friends clearly is not my concern. What I've realized now and

probably was underlying all along is that the issues our industry face are actually part of a much bigger situation.

I really wish this had a happier ending, but right now, it just doesn't. I'm not going to pretend. This is why this write up never got to the Publisher.

What can we do? How can we go about things in a more ethical and kinder way and become smarter about what we are doing? How can we do it in a cleaner, more "Humane", more sustainable way?

Can we? And if not... should we?

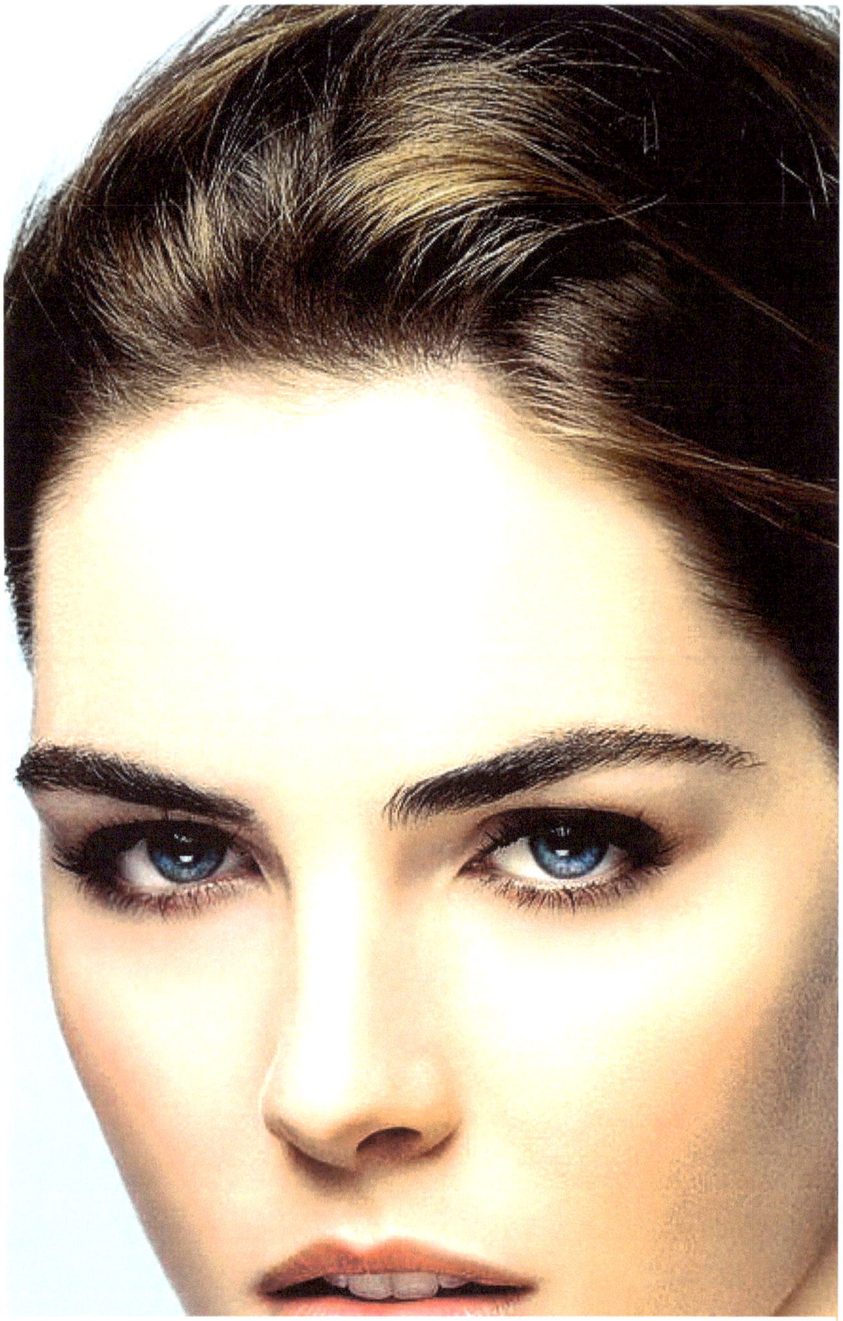

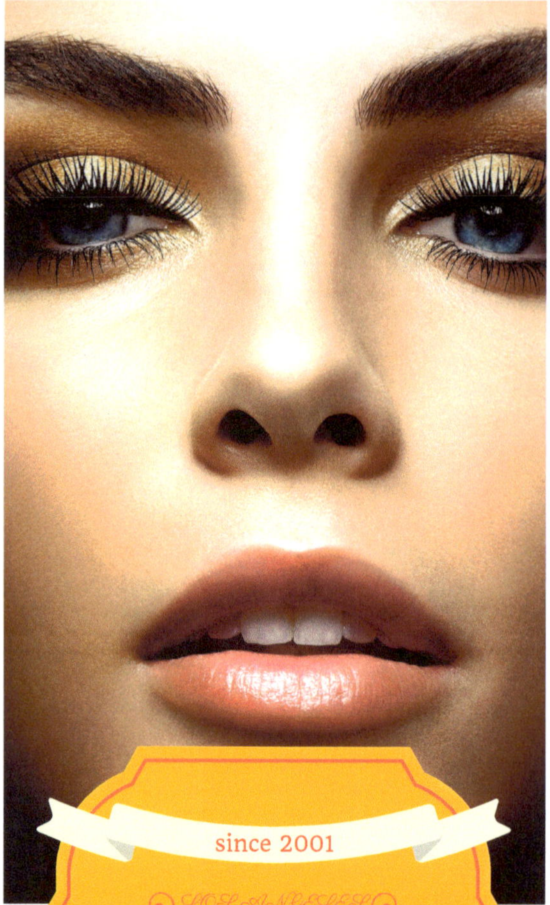

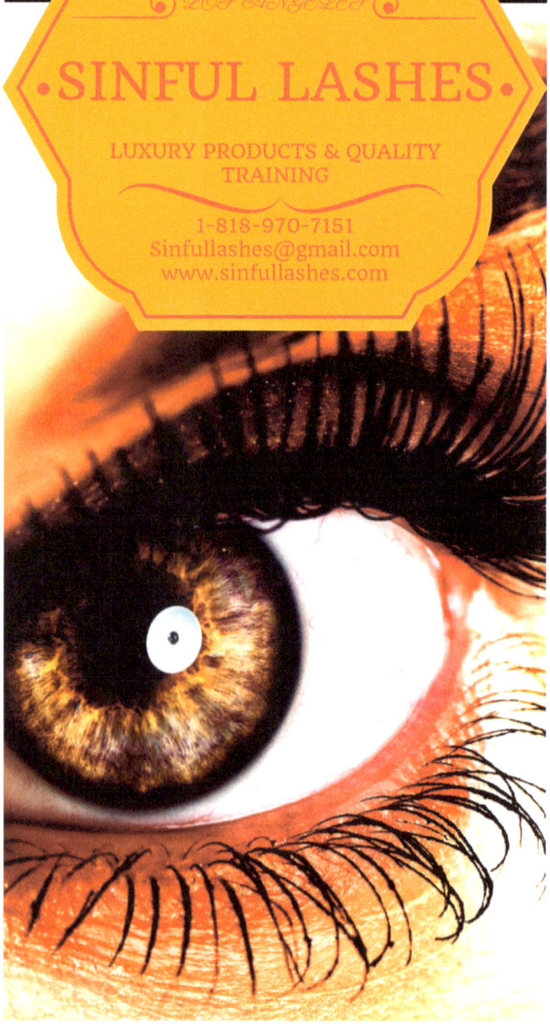

LUXURY PRODUCTS AT COMPETITIVE PRICES. FEATURING OUR RED RUBY VOLUME ADHESIVE

Sinful Lashes

QUALITY, IN-DEPTH TRAINING LOCATED IN LOS ANGELES. WE ALSO TRAVEL THE US BRINGING OUR CLASSIC AND VOLUME TRAINING TO YOU

SUMMER TRENDS
VIBRANT COLOUR

Fashion influences cosmetics and what clients request. So with this season being all about the tropics and bold colours what can you do to add some vibrancy into your lashing?

Fantasy lashes are a huge thing in countries such as Russia and the Ukraine with competitions held several times per year. It is also very popular in the USA with more suppliers offering colour lashes, accessories and training courses.

Here in the UK, where we tend to be more conservative, a bit un-adventurous, it is not a massively requested for service (yet). Decorating lashes at the moment happens mainly at make up competitions or as part of college make up courses.

But, there is massive potential to offer bespoke creations for your clients, to match their lashes to their hair colour, shoes, nails, clothes or for a special event.

If you haven't considered using coloured lashes or offering eye adornments for your clients perhaps now is the time. Look for a good training provider with a range of lash supplies to take your creations to a new level.

Lashes by Barcsai-Gáspár Orsolya

CARRIE FUELL

Sugar Lash
Colour Lashes

Tanja Nicklaus

@Sandrakarlssons
Lash4Lash

Tanja Nicklaus

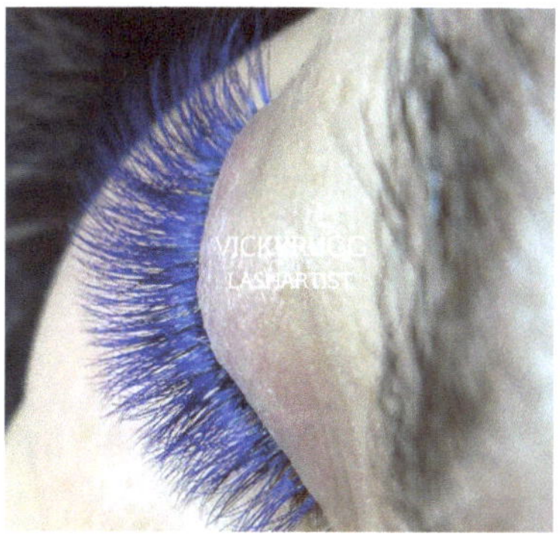

VICKIEWIGS
LASHARTIST

Tanja Nicklaus

Michelle Ryan

WHAT IS VOLUME?

Kim Jaynes & Erin Taylor

What is Volume lashing? Russian volume technique is the pristine method of safely applying anywhere from 2 to 6 super fine, lightweight extensions per natural lash. With the classic lash technique, you can only apply one extension to one natural lash, meaning we can only work with what we've got! This can be disappointing to some clients who have very few lashes but want a full look.

Many who have heard about the new volume technique have had various questions involving the health of the natural eyelashes. Is it too heavy? Are you overloading the lash line? Will it damage my lashes? But with training and understanding of this new technique, you can actually apply more lashes using less weight. You can also use a smaller amount of adhesive because it adheres to more surface area of the natural lash. It almost wraps around the entire natural lash, coating it in the adhesive, giving the fan a stronger hold while still maintaining the flexibility of the natural lash.

What's the difference between volume and clusters? There is a big difference between volume lashing and cluster lashes. For those who are new to understanding this technique, we'd like to clear up a few of those questions:

Volume Lashing is indeed a technique, not a type of lash. It's the process of creating a fan or a bouquet made from individual lashes, with various diameters. They are applied to one isolated natural lash. Therefore, the fan cycles out properly with the natural lash cycle

and new lashes grow healthily in their place. Be weary of those who are not trained in volume and try to use thicker diameters to create this look, for it will cause major damage.

Cluster/Flare Lashes are a quick, easy way to apply groups of pre-made clumps or cluster fans to the base of the natural lash line. They are bound together at the base of their fans with a little knot of plastic material to hold anywhere from 4-7 synthetic fibers into a V shape. These lashes are extremely heavy and are applied to the base of the natural lashes with no proper isolation. They should not be applied or worn long-term. People often forget the natural lashes go through a cycle, making it very difficult for proper lash cycling to take place when the lashes are all glued together. This can be a very dangerous and harmful technique to the natural lashes when done improperly.

Borboleta Beauty's Method: Nowadays, there are many different artists and trainers around the world who have come up with their own unique way to create the Russian volume fans. At Borboleta, we firmly believe there is not one right way to do volume. Of course you have to take into account the weight of the lashes being applied, the amount of glue you are using, as well as eyelash isolation, but ultimately we are all trying to achieve the same end result. Through tedious wrist movements and different amounts of pressure applied, we can all create our volume fans in a unique way. This does not mean any fan works for volume just because it looks like a fan. There are different ways to achieve our fans, but there are still guidelines we need to follow when creating our Russian Volume look.

ABOUT BORBOELTA BEAUTY BY KIM JAYNES

When developing Borboleta Beauty's product line, I wanted to achieve two things: top quality eyelash extensions and strong adhesives that were safe. As a lash artist, I hated the plastic-feeling, fake-looking, and lose-their-curl-in-a-few-days lashes. I wanted soft, flexible and human like extensions that had women asking themselves, "Are her lashes real? They're perfection!"

After finding the perfect lashes, I was on a mission to find flexible, strong glue with safe ingredients. Who wants to adhere beautiful lashes with yucky glue? Not me! Borboleta's adhesives have been broken down by a chemist, who then helped us purify the formula. We removed harsh chemicals like formaldahyde and latex -- while still maintaining a formula with beautiful hold and flexibility -- so our lash artists could avoid red, watery eyes and intense allergic reactions.

At Borboleta Beauty, we let you have your cake and eat it too! With passion for beauty and brains, we've created an incredible training program and an equally high-quality product line. And we're proud of it!

BE HAPPY AND MAKE OTHERS HAPPY

The cold weather is behind us and it's time to shake off those winter blues and find something better to talk about with our clients than the snow. The time you spend with your clients is not just valuable in terms of income or beauty, but it's also an opportunity to spread a little positively and joy. If you want to be successful, realize that your own personal happiness is always key. It will allow you to be successful in your career, your friendships, and in your relationships.

Pick a few interesting and uplifting topics to focus on when talking with your clients and avoid going down the path of gossip or complaining. Not only will you feel better and more refreshed at the end of the day, but your clients will also leave inspired and with a more positive frame of mind. What an amazing win-win! Be a contributor to the solution rather than to the problem. Having your energy sucked dry by complaints and clients spilling personal dramas will inevitably wear on you and could even cause fatigue, depression, and anxiety.

Make it a point every day, with every person, to create inspiration and joy within them and pay it forward in the process of attaining success and happiness in your own life.

Let's face it: We're all dispensable. Anybody can do what you do, but it's the way in which you do it that will create uniqueness and will draw people to you specifically and make the services that you provide indispensable. Have integrity, speak diplomatically, be a mentor, and be the absolute best you can be. Be unique and share your passion and joy and good things will be drawn to you like a magnet.

"Earned success" is one of the primary ways that we receive joy. There are many studies that have been conducted proving that money is not what makes a successful person happy. Rather, it is the earned success itself. It's not

about the amount of money you make; it's about the perception of being successful and earning it on your own that truly brings joy. We are all very lucky in the beauty industry to be able to bring joy and happiness into other people's lives as an integral part of our career. Being able to interact with people on a daily basis gives you the opportunity to bring joy into their lives, which, in turn, improves your level of happiness.

Though it is often described as one, it is no "secret" that keeping a positive frame of mind is what ultimately will bring all the success in

the world straight to your front door. Yet the problem does not lie solely in understanding that a positive frame of mind is what will bring you success. In short, the problem is not failing to arrive at that positive frame of mind; the problem is maintaining it. It is difficult, sometimes, to steer clients away from negativity, so strategize your conversation starters and always try to find a sliver lining for them. (For some inspiration, check out larowbeautygroup.com.)

To summarize, the key to success is happiness, and the key to happiness is success. Take care of yourself and surround yourself with people who help you to maintain your positive frame of mind, your passion, your motivation, and your dream.

Best Lashes!
Leah Lynch
Mentor/Educator

MACULAR DEGENERATION

Macular degeneration is a painless eye condition which usually occurs with age. It causes vision to become increasingly blurry and makes colours appear less vibrant. Because it doesn't affect peripheral vision, it can't cause a complete loss of sight. While macular degeneration usually affects both eyes, the speed of progression can significantly vary. Loss of vision is very slow and usually occurs over the course of many years. It's currently the leading cause of visual impairment in the UK and tends to be more common among women than men.

SYMPTOMS

All macular degeneration symptoms are related to quality of sight. Blurred vision and difficulty distinguishing faces are the most common issues. In serious occurrences, blind spots or hallucinations may also occur directly in the middle of the visual field. Less serious symptoms usually occur between five and 10 years before visuals are affected. These include sensitivity to light, colours appearing less vibrant and hazy outbreaks. When symptoms develop, medical treatment should be sought at the earliest possible convenience.

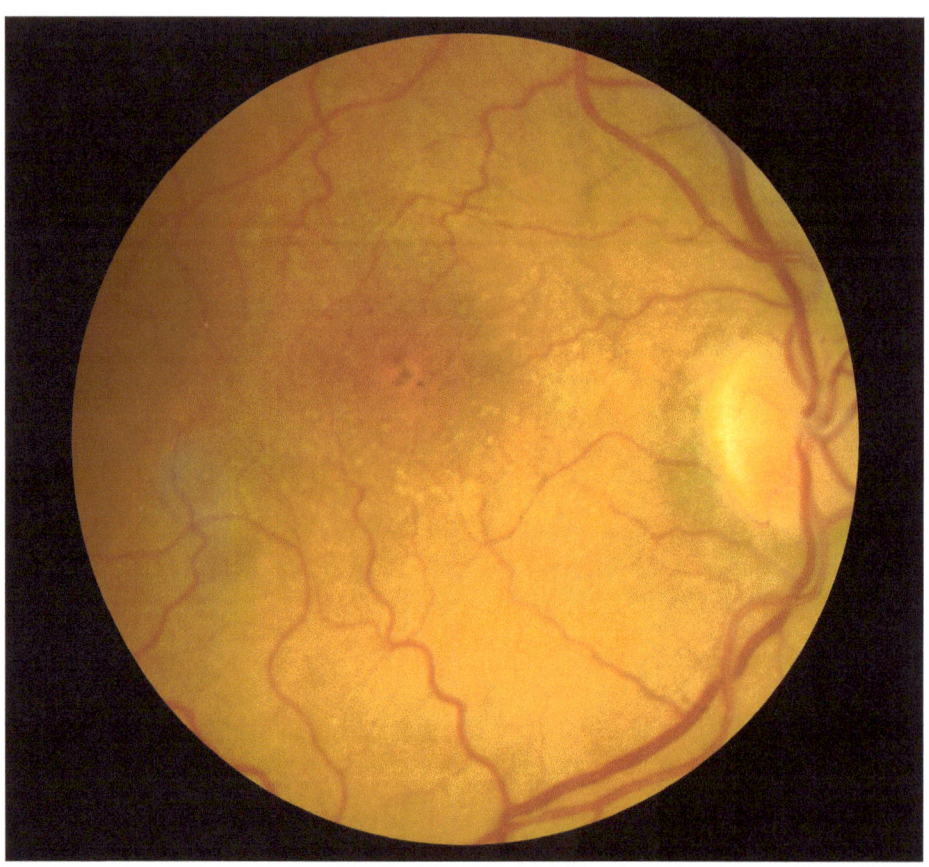

A Fundus photo showing Macular Degeneration (Back of Eye).

TREATMENT

There is currently no cure for macular degeneration. Treatment usually revolves around helping individual's make the most out of the vision they have with glasses and contact lenses. Some evidence suggests that consumption of leafy green vegetables can prolong macular degeneration. Early diagnosis is often essential when preventing severe loss of vision as the condition can be treated with anti-VEGF medication; this stops it from getting worse. In some instances laser eye surgery can be used to destroy abnormal blood vessels.

FLASHES AND FLOATERS

Flashes and floaters are very common and can occur either together or separately. They are often a complaint among the elderly and are usually attributed to the collapse of vitreous gel. However, there are also more serious causes as well, such as retinal detachment.

Flashes (photopsia) occur when the individual sees flashing lights – like a lightbulb switching on and off in quick succession. They are primarily caused by two reasons; improper stimulation of the retina and problems with the optic nerve.

Floaters are opacities that float in the sufferer's field of vision. They are usually seen as spots or wavy lines. They move with eye movements and will often disperse when the patient looks at them directly. There are a number of causes for floaters such as ageing, vitreous detachment, inflammatory cells and tumours. In around 25% of circumstances, no underlying causes are found. Most people tend to ignore floaters and get used to them after time.

SYMPTOMS

Typical symptoms of flashes include seeing lights, stars and halos. While symptoms of floaters usually revolve around seeing shapes, they can lead to headaches when the patient focuses on them.

TREATMENT

In most circumstances flashes and floaters won't require any treatment and will fade over the course of time. Vitamin therapy may cause them to disappear, however, even this is rarely recommended. Vitreous floaters may be caused by a tear in the retina; this may require surgery to prevent the retina from detaching from the eye.

CRAB LICE

Crab lice (crabs) are usually found in the pubic or genital area of humans; however, they can also be found in other areas where course hair grows, such as the eyebrows and eyelashes. Crab lice are usually spread through sexual contact, but can also be transmitted through close contact of clothing, bedding and towels. Crab lice can be difficult to find because they are usually few in number. Infestation is diagnosed when eggs (nits) are found. The lifecycle of crab lice is between 16 and 25 days, and females lay around three eggs per day. Crab lice feed exclusively on blood at least four to five times per day. During these times symptoms become more severe.

SYMPTOMS

Symptoms usually appear between five and seven days after infestation. The primary symptom is itching. This usually gets worse during the night as the lice become more active. Scratching often causes inflammations and redness. Blue spots may also occur from the biting.

TREATMENT

Over-the-counter shampoos and conditioners are the most common treatment. Doctors may also prescribe lindane shampoo, which is more aggressive and rarely recommended as the first line of treatment. After treatment, affected individuals should always wear clean underwear and clothing, and avoid sexual contact for at least two weeks.

DISTICHIASIS

Distichiasis is a rare condition which causes two rows of eyelashes to grow. The extra row grows from the meibomian glands and can protrude into the cornea and cause serious corneal abrasions. There are two types of distichiasis; acquired and congenital. With acquired distichiasis, lashes form specifically on the lower eyelids. The congenital form is usually inherited.

SYMPTOMS

Many sufferers don't have symptoms and may not even be aware of their condition. However, in most circumstances the affected eye will become red and inflamed. Some people experience the feeling of having something constantly stuck in their eye.

TREATMENT

It's important to treat distichiasis as soon as possible as the eyelash could scratch the surface of the eye and cause other more serious problems. Ophthalmic lubricants without preservatives can protect the cornea; however, this is only a short term solution as they must be applied between three and four times per day. Cryotherapy is often used to freeze the hair follicules to -20 degrees, which results in permanent removal. Laser treatments may also be used.

LASH LIFT

Leanne Bolton

Hi, my name is Leanne Bolton and I'm the owner of Hello Gorgeous Training Academy. I have been lashing for 9 years and I believe the lash lift treatment is a fantastic opportunity to increase your client base and profit.

The benefits of lash lift:-
• Suitable for all lashes
• Lasts 6-8 weeks
• No Adhesives/Mascara required
• Natural looking
• Lifts very straight lashes which allow for easier bonding of individual or volume lashes

STEP 1
Ensure you have your kit to hand which includes all the essential products.
Cleanse your eyelashes with the protein pads and you're ready to go.

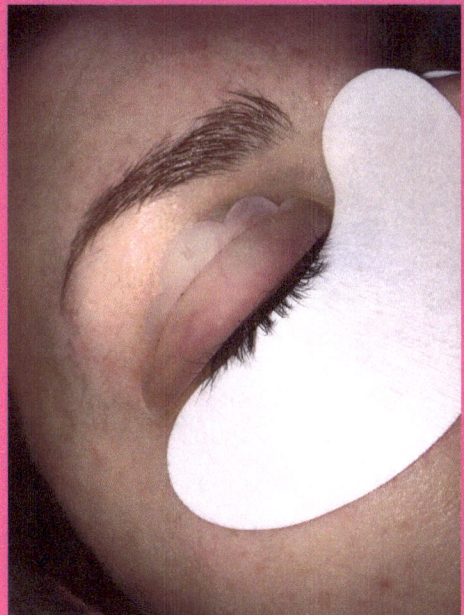 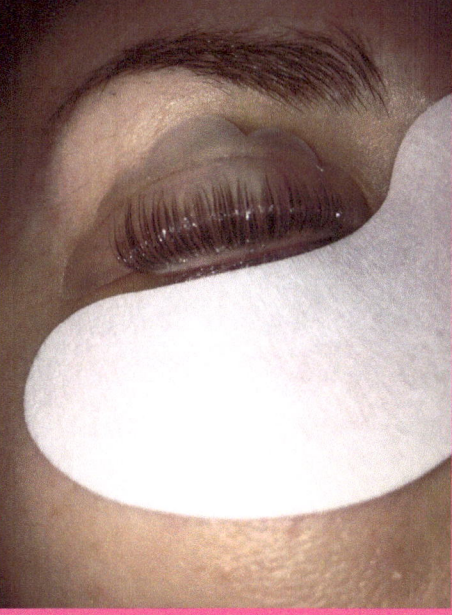 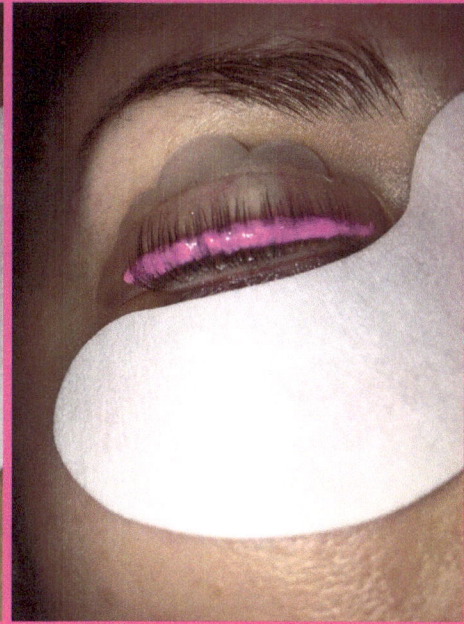

STEP 2 & 3

Tape down the lower lashes with your under eye gel pads.
Choose the correct shield size for your Client and apply just above the lash line.

STEP 4

Pull back the upper lashes on to the shield using the lash lift separating tool.

STEP 5

Apply the perming lotion.
Wait for the correct amount of time before removing the perming lotion.

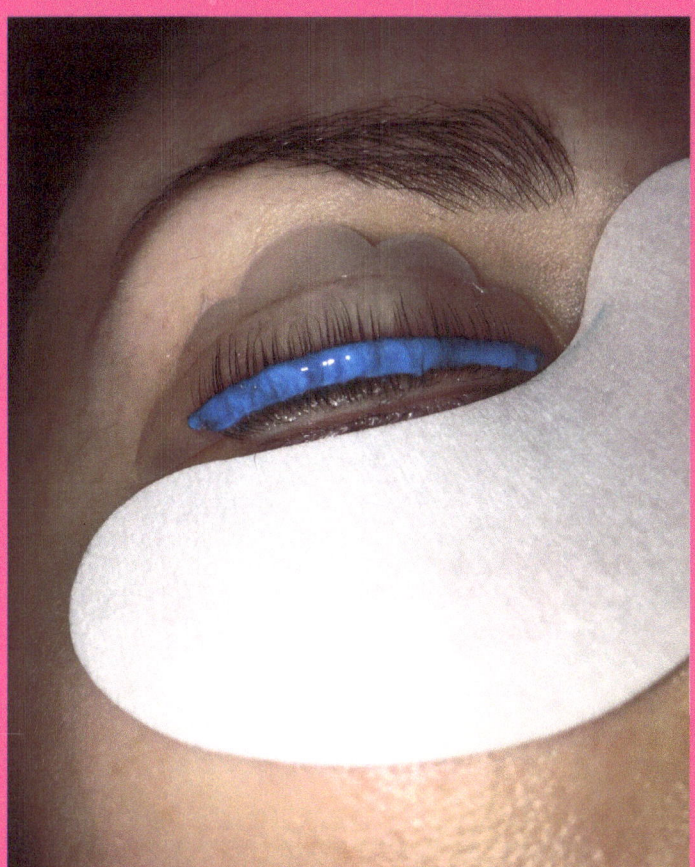 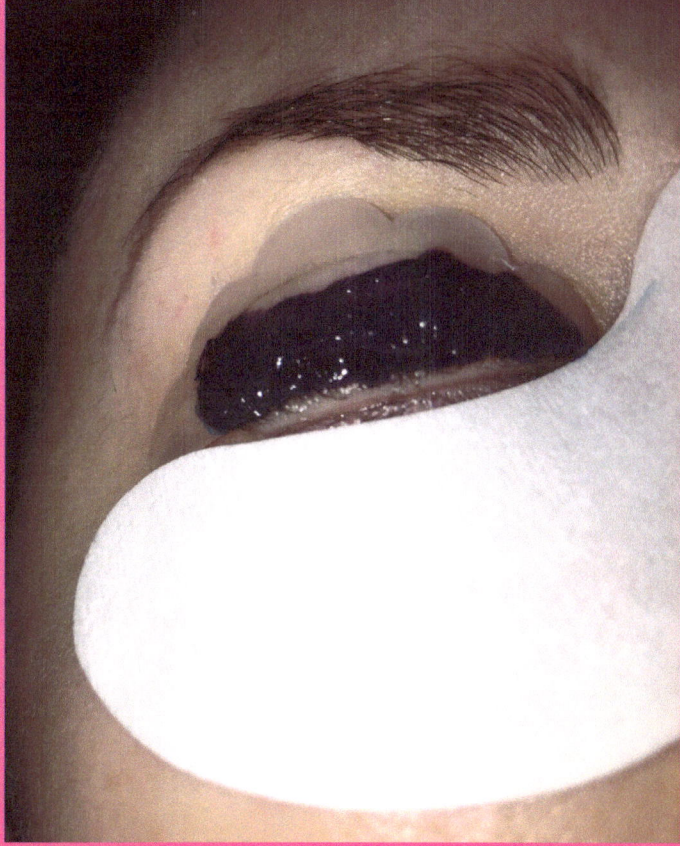

STEP 6

Apply the fixing lotion.
Wait for the correct amount of time before removing the fixing lotion.

STEP 7 & 8

Apply the tint to the lashes to give a colour boost.
Remove the tint and apply the nourishing lotion to help lift the lashes from the shield.

LASH INC THERAPISTS

Pioneering insurance package specifically designed for you

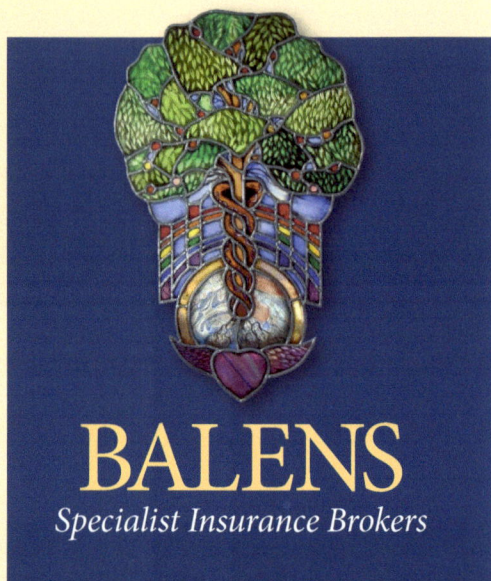

BALENS
Specialist Insurance Brokers

LASH INC INSURANCE PACKAGE

- » £6m Medical Malpractice
- » £6m Professional Indemnity
- » £6m Public & Products Liability cover
- » Taxation and Legal Package
- » Student to student / Case study cover

PREMIUM FROM

£74

PER YEAR *(Incl. Taxes & Fees)*

Teaching is included in this package as standard, however, if you are delivering your own qualification, have over 20 students or a turnover in excess of £20,000 per annum, you may need a Training School policy.

'Please quote **Lash14** for your 10% premium discount on your Training School policy'

Pioneers for over 60 years!
Caring for the carers

Telephone: 01684 580 771
Web: www.balens.co.uk
Email: info@balens.co.uk

Balens Ltd is Authorised and Regulated by the Financial Conduct Authority.

Q & A

with

DAVID BALEN - Balens Specialist Insurance Brokers

Do you want to understand insurance better?

Insurance is often viewed quite negatively, but it can be the difference between losing your livelihood or not, whilst being essential in promoting a professional image to the outer world along with protecting the public. In today's claims culture aided by the rise of "no win, no fee" solicitors, the ability to sue is no longer restricted to the rich or famous. If you carry out a treatment or give advice regardless to whom or how frequent, you are at risk!

Q: How can individual therapists protect themselves?

A: "I would recommend ensuring that you have a good quality Insurance to help protect against clients or others who may chose to make a claim or complain. Cover should include Public Liability, Medical Malpractice, Breach of Confidentiality, Financial Loss, Criminal and Tax defence, Loss of Reputation and Products Liability. If you don't have an adequate wording, you could find yourself held financially liable if it were proved that it was your advice or treatment, or the products used that were responsible for the clients' alleged situation. There are of course other types of protection available that can cover; Contents, buildings, items taken away from the premises e.g mobile equipment and laptops, loss of profits arising from damage to your clinic premises, protecting yourself or colleagues for loss of income due to illness, accident or death and so on. For corporate entities with multi therapist clinics, businesses selling health products or other commercial ventures, there are various special packages available.

If you are teaching and/or issuing your own qualifications you may also require an additional policy"

Q: Are there any common pitfalls in this?

A: "I would say that most of the pitfalls we experience are due to a therapist's lack of knowledge, or from not letting insurers know of any material facts or changes relevant to the risks being insured. As an example if you start working from home, you need to advise your home insurer about this, if they were not previously informed. Many home insurance providers do not cover working from home and they may choose to refuse a claim, even an unrelated one, if they discover you have been working from home and they were unaware of it. Other common pitfalls include individuals under insuring themselves (i.e. taking out cover for their business contents for less than its value), and when the business becomes slightly larger with more therapists working in the same place, they do not grow their insurance cover with the business. i.e. they believe they will be adequately covered by their own individual Professional Indemnity insurances rather than getting a corporate policy.

This is not always the case, and practitioners should always seek professional advice on what cover they need at every stage of their business' development. There can also be confusion as to how long cover will last if discontinuing a policy.

Some types of policy are on a "claims made" basis and may not continue cover for an adequate period after terminating, or indeed, at all! Some do not pick up previous work performed under another policy when changing insurer. These are key elements to check when choosing your insurance products"

Q: What are the most common complaints?

A: "Many complaints arise within the first few sessions with a new client, and often result from misunderstandings, miscommunication, and inadequate advice given at the outset. Failing to manage a client's expectations or inappropriate behaviour can also be cause for complaint.

Remember to:

~ Keep your boundaries,

~ Show good listening and communication skills

~ Never claim or imply that you are able to cure a condition

~ Manage the clients' expectations regarding your services: including cost, length of time it could take

~ Explain both the possible positive and possible negative effects of the treatment.

Remember to keep good records (for at least 7 years – preferably indefinitely) of what you have told the client, your records are your first line of defence if a claim is made against you. Choosing a Broker with a good track record in giving expert and sympathetic claims support is vital."

Q: What should a therapist do if a claim is made against them?

A: "First don't panic. Contact your Broker; they should be able to give advice on how best to deal with the situation. Never admit liability or promise to pay, this prejudices your insurers position, and may mean that your insurance becomes nullified. There are ways of dealing with this. If in doubt, ask. We all make mistakes, it is part of being human, but with good quality support you can be reassured that you will not be paying the price of that mistake yourself: you can then reflect, learn and move on".

For further information including articles and online CPD films see www.balens.co.uk/education

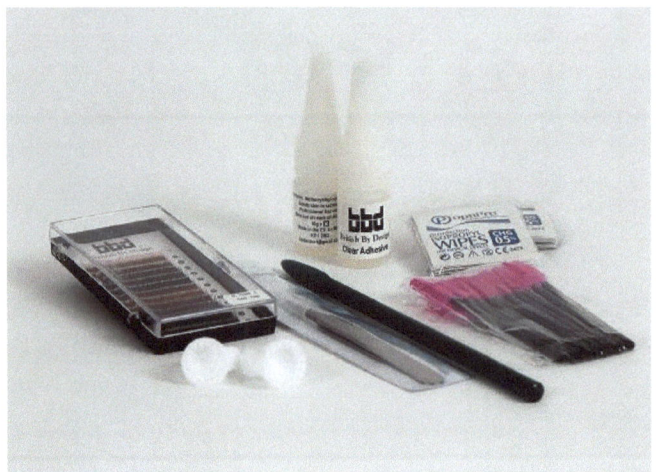

BBD BROWS

BBD Eyebrow extensions have moved from monthly eyelash extension classes to weekly eyebrow extension training courses in Glasgow to cope with increased demand. BBD offer affordable training and eyebrow extension kits, which is ideal if you are looking to take on this treatment.

bbdexport@gmail.com

NEW TWIST ON SALON TREATMENT

NSL inch loss wraps have now launched an inch loss massage candle. The candle is a new twist on their classic inch loss body treatment. Light the candle allow the product to melt, pour into your hand and cover the clients skin. The client is then wrapped with Spa film wrap and rests for 45 minutes while the product works. The result a slimmer client with soft and nourished skin.
www.nslwrap.com

NOUVEAU LASHES FREE TRAINING UK

Nouveau lashes are a well respected supplier and training provider. They recently launched their new branding and along side their free training offer.
To view their offer please call 0844 801 6824 or visit
http://nouveaulashes.com/

ELLIPSE LASHES

The flat base of these types of lashes means you can offer a much fuller look without adding the usual weight of a thicker extension. Another added benefit is that the flat base offers a larger surface area to create a strong and longer lasting bond between the extension and natural lash. Some companies also emboss the flat base so that they are rougher and can potentially last even longer. Just out are super lightweight Ellipse lashes with 'Nano holes' creating a lash that is very light however it will not 'suck up' glue making it heavy due to the size of these microscopic holes.

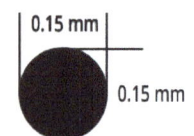

Normal Eyelash Extensions   **Ellipse 'Flat Lash' Eyelash Extension**

Flat based lashes also known as Ellipse lashes are becoming a favourite with many salons, the ease of application and the promise of increased retention makes them a summer 'must try'.

NOVALASH 24 HOUR SHADOWS COMPLEMENT LASH EXTENSION SERVICES

Perfect for weddings, holidays, beach & everyday wear

NovaLash extends its 'effortless beauty' philosophy with award-winning 24 Hour Cream Shadow Triptychs. Already loved by UK makeup artists, these waterproof, extended-wear cream eye shadow formulas will not crease or smudge for over 24 hours. They also will not leave a messy, powdery dust on lash extensions, as can happen with traditional eye shadows.

If a business or makeup artist currently have clients with lash extensions, it is a smart move to retail this new line as customers who enjoy the benefits of wearing lash extensions will also enjoy the same

benefits of the 24 Hour Shadows—easy, effortless, smudge-proof wear. The shadows are unique in the market and will enhance the benefits of wearing lash extensions while growing retail profits. Each kit retails for £37.

http://www.novalash.com/uk/

We are now taking new applications for Lash Inc accreditaion. The accreditation will show potential students your materials are of a set standard and that your qualifications have been verified. Students are looking for peace of mind and accreditation can help with this.

For details please visit **http://www.lashinc.eu/**

LASH INC IRELAND

Lash Inc Journal is now available for Irish lash artists. This customised version will cover Irish trends, training and news as well as the international features.

www.lashincireland.com

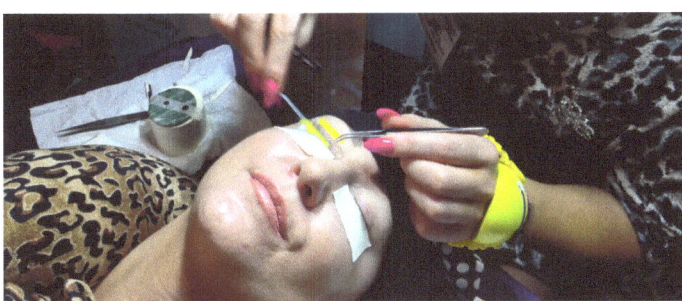

The national event returns...

BeautyUK back at the NEC this May

The BeautyUK experience returns to the NEC Birmingham this May, showcasing more than 600 brands over two days.

Taking place on Sunday 10th and Monday 11th May, the event combines the best equipment, product and treatment launches from the Beauty, Nails, Tanning, and Spa sectors, and runs alongside NailsUK, HairUK, BarberUK and Holistic Health to create the national beauty trade event in the heart of the UK.

By registering for free tickets, you can join over 25,000 other industry professionals to discuss the latest industry buzz, share knowledge, network with like-minded salon owners, therapists and lash technicians, and take home the very latest professional products and equipment.

For make-up artists and lash technicians in particular, there's a wealth of exhibitors that you may be interested in from Artdeco, Airbase and Benefit Cosmetics through to Angel Eyes, Lash Perfect, Vanity Lash and Blinc Inc to name but a few. Plus, you can pick up salon essentials from names such as Lycon Precision Wax and Your Salon Store, and get your uniforms sorted with La Beeby.

Of course, no show would be complete without special offers and thanks to the generosity of our exhibitors, BeautyUK visitors can make great savings for their business simply by taking advantage of our exclusive show-only deals. And if you're interested in CPD, there'll be a host of beauty, nail and holistic therapy training experts on hand to discuss your educational options to really help build your career.

ABT Seminar Programme

Supported by therapists' membership organisation ABT, the Seminar Programme at BeautyUK is held completely free of charge to all visitors. Here you'll find inspiring talks and demonstrations on a wide range of topics including treatment techniques, advice on running your salon business and information sessions on industry news.

Take a seat at any time during the two days of BeautyUK and leave inspired with ideas and changes for your business and career.

Habia / VTCT Live Stage

If that wasn't enough, there'll be a wealth of expert advice on hand from the Habia Skills Team and their education experts on the Habia / VTCT Live Stage, with topics ranging from how to build your business through to filling your skills gaps.

Plus, visit the Habia / VTCT stand to receive one-to-one advice on your individual business concerns or CPD options.

NATIONAL MUA AWARDS

National Make-up Artist Awards 2015

Join us for the second annual National Make-up Artist Awards as it expands to become a two-day competition. Entries are open now for Professional and Student make-up artists to take part, showcasing their skills to the industry-leading judging panel. Awards are presented to winners in each category, with prizes including professional make-up and the opportunity to assist the Artdeco Creativ team at a red carpet event or photoshoot.

REGISTER FOR FREE TICKETS

Tickets to BeautyUK are completely free for trade professionals when booked in advance, saving the £20 registration fee on the day. Register online at www.BeautyUKShow.com or by calling the ticket hotline on 01332 227 698.

Your ticket will be sent out around 7-10 days before the event, and gives access to the show on both Sunday 10th and Monday 11th May, plus free entry to the NailsUK, HairUK, BarberUK and Holistic Health exhibitions.

As entry is free, why not invite your colleagues to join you at this national event?

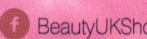 BeautyUKShow ⓕ BeautyUKShow

#BeautyUK15

5 SHOWS · **600** BRANDS · **2** DAYS · **1** VENUE

BEAUTY UK · **NAILS** UK · **HAIR** UK
BARBER UK · **HOLISTIC** HEALTH

Beauty

BACK TO BASICS EYEBROW SHAPING

Ruth Morrison

Eyebrow shaping is probably one of the most common treatments therapists will carry out, and although eyebrows are a small proportion of your facial features, they are super important, and can completely change the appearance of someone's face.

To decide what kind of shape would suit the client, and flatter their face shape, we first need to determine what face shape the client has. It might be easier to pull the hair from the client's face, in which case a hair band is useful to have to hand, this way the client can still lie comfortably on your beauty bed.

There are 6 basic face shapes that we can work from, oval, round, long, square heart and diamond.

With your clients hair pulled back off the face we can decide what face shape they have, to help determine this should you be unsure, there are some observations that can be made......

Oval shape – client will have visible and predominant cheek bones, their forehead will be wider than their chin and the lower part of their face will gradually taper to a narrow chin.
Round shape – as suggested, a round shape will appear round with the face being dimensionally very similar in length of face and the width of the face, it is common that the face will probably be widest at the cheek area.

Long shape – while the chin are is similar to an oval shape, narrowing down to a nice tapered narrow chin, a long face is similar in width at the forehead, cheekbones and jawline.

Square shape – this face shape is similar to a long face shape, being of similar width at forehead, cheekbones and jawline, but from the jawline to the chin area there is very little length, squaring the facial shape as opposed to tapering down to a longer point with the long face shape.

Diamond shape – the widest point of this facial shape will be the highest point of the cheekbones, almost eye level, normally the forehead area will not be very large and the face tapers down to a pointed chin area from the widest point. Features are very angular with this face shape.

There are a few different eyebrow shapes, and these shapes can be altered in thickness (should the client have adequate eyebrow hair

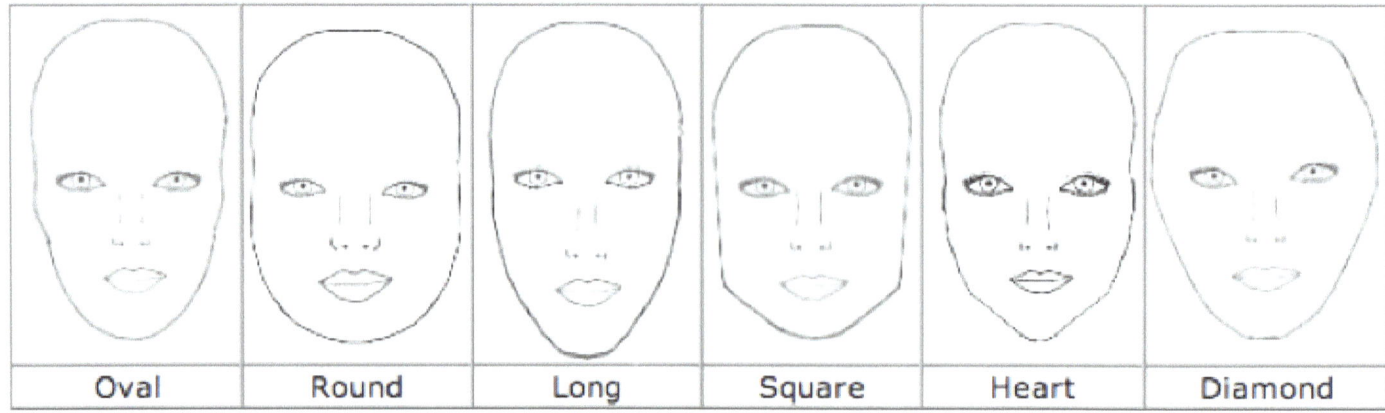

| Oval | Round | Long | Square | Heart | Diamond |

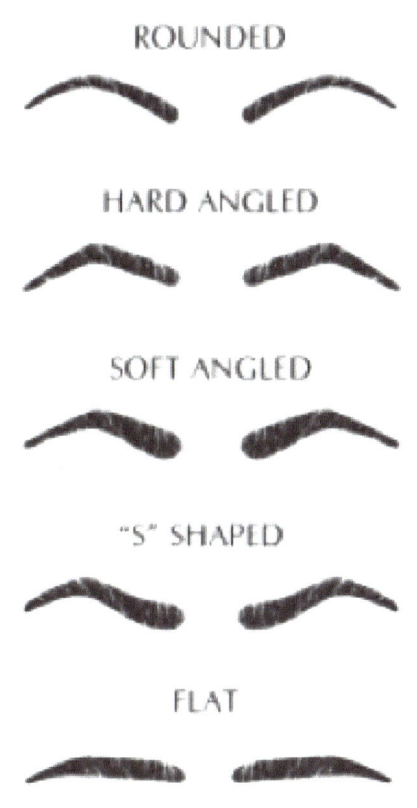

ROUNDED

HARD ANGLED

SOFT ANGLED

"S" SHAPED

FLAT

to work with, failing this make up can be used to complete the look)

How do we decide what face shape will suit our clients? A basic rule is a shape that will balance out and compliment the client's facial shape.

Oval shaped clients are very lucky, with great proportion's most shapes will suit this facial shape, and so you can discuss what shapes are preferred, and complete the treatment, a soft angled shape is great should the client want any suggestions.

Round shaped clients will benefit from a shape that will not emphasise this facial shape, we want to make the face appear longer, and so a hard angled eyebrow will break up the roundness of the face and help the face to appear longer.

Long faced clients benefit from a shape that will help to make the face look shorter, so we want to create the illusion of width in the eyebrow area, to do this the flat shape is complimentary and does not create any extra height that would only emphasise the long shape of the face.

Square shaped clients have 2 options, the face can be softened, as discussed earlier this facial shape is very angular, and can benefit from a

rounded eyebrow shape to soften these features or, the face can be balanced by giving them a soft angled brow which works with the angles of the jawline, these options can be discussed with your client.

Heart shaped clients are similar to square shaped clients, and have predominant and visible angular features, clients with a hear shape suit rounded brows to soften these features, the rounded shape can be very soft and not too high, but a high rounded shape can be created to vary the effect.

Diamond shaped clients are pretty far and few between, this is not a common face shape and benefits from softening the angular features that come with this face shape, to do this we need to create a soft rounded shape, we can also create a very soft angled shape, with not a lot of height.

When discussing these options with your client, to give them an idea of how the shape suggested will look, you can use an eyebrow pencil to pencil in the shape over your client's natural brow, this will let your client see what you propose to remove, and give them an idea of the final shape. When client's need a little help in certain area's why not have some eyebrow products available to retail? After demonstrating how they are used with your own personal kit, clients can see how well they work, and you can retail your chosen brand, upselling to an eyebrow tint before shaping is a great way of adding extra depth to the final look.

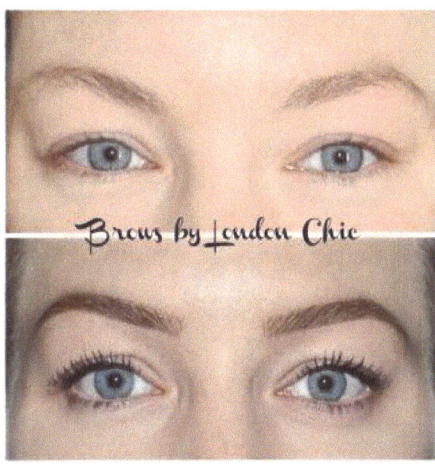

Brows by London Chic

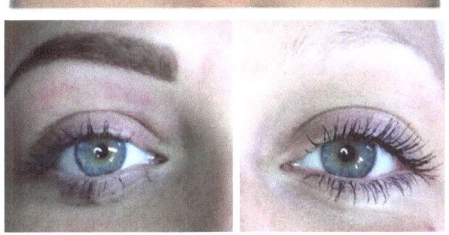

Kim Monique Tonnesen

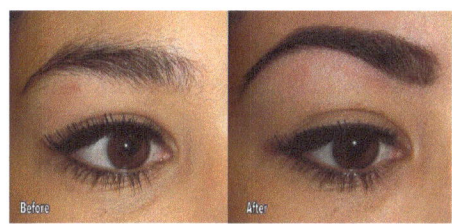

Becky Perkins

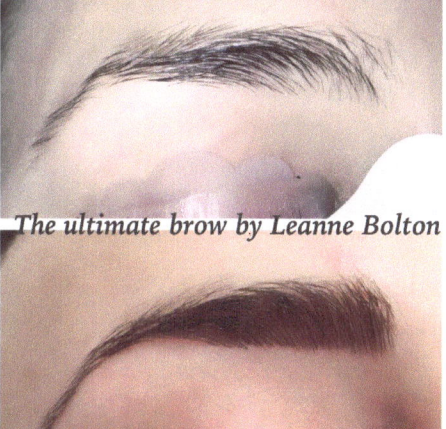

The ultimate brow by Leanne Bolton

HD BROWS

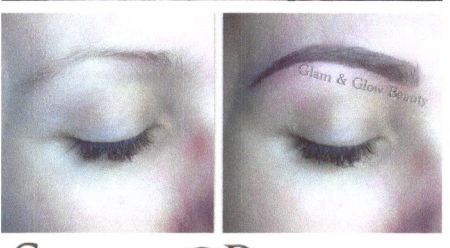

SLEEK BROWS
3D BROW BUILDING

BEAUTY EDIT

MelVicMakeup has been a busy bee in the makeup world recently and is going to be even busier in the future with lots of exciting projects about to be launched! I will soon be back working on the set of Downton Abby where I will be taking along some of my students that I have taught in the past to give them a real insight into the world of makeup on a TV set and where better to do it than the best Drama in the world, I will share more about our days on set very soon....

Once again I was asked to body art for the Chic Networking Event to give my student makeup artists a taste of what it is like backstage; this event was in the Hilton Hotel Liverpool and was a fashion and lifestyle event for all the family, I took along some of my students to help out at the event to help them gain real industry work experience and great portfolio pictures, we did use lashes for the catwalk models and the body art models, however the catwalk models had mascara only in the end as the look was clumpy lashes but the body art girls had some beautiful Red Cherry lashes that stood out fabulously.

Photography: Andrew Harrison: 07588557822 Website: www.facebook.com/Andrewharrisonphotography

Battle of the mascaras...

PERRON RIGOT - BROW SCULPTOR EYEBROW KIT

I have been trialling a number of mascaras and the best ones that I have found are 'Le Maq Pro Mascara' in black and 'CODE Beautiful Mascara' also in black. I have worn the mascaras for a number of different events including a long day at the Professional Beauty Show in London, exercising in the gym to my occasional power walk which lately has been in the freezing cold and rain! Each of the mascaras did well, both are sweat proof and they each have their own unique selling points......

MASCARAS
Price range from £8.21 to £10.26, which is really reasonable and affordable to most clientele, they are available in a range of colours also. Available from Twitter @ LeMaqPro on 01514211234 or **www.LeMaqPro.com**

CLASSIC LE MAQ PRO MASCARAS

Le Maq Pro has been around for 30 years and is manufactured in France and use high quality raw materials from natural sources. All mascaras have a tapered end to the brush, allowing easy access to the inner corner of the eye and also suitable for small eyes yet still a big enough wand to cater for all other eye shapes providing curl, definition and separation. The unique selling point to this mascara is the wand that is 'C' shaped to allow easy application to all the lashes in one go and for makeup artists who have to use disposables, you get a good amount of mascara on the wand to be able to transfer to the disposable wand, which can sometimes be a real pain with other mascaras that I have tried and tested. There is a waterproof version in the black however I found the non-waterproof one lasted really well throughout the day. I would have to say that this mascara wins for the makeup artist as the transfer of product is so easy and it dries really quickly so no transferring once the client looks up!

Not tested on animals and Paraben free

Price £19.95 for a very generous 12ml, Available from Harvey Nichols, QVC, Beauty Bay and selected stylish salons. www.code-beautiful.com, Twitter @ codebeautiful

CODE BEAUTIFUL

After tweaking and testing the formula this mascara has now found a perfect combination of ingredients that really effectively lift the lashes and lengthen them like no other mascara I have ever used before! It is almost like fiber mascara without the clumps that you tend to get with fiber style mascaras. I would say this is one of my favorites for the everyday woman who has very short lashes or thin wispy lashes and needs an added volume boost. The unique selling point for this mascara has to be the instant lengthening that you get after just a couple of sweeps of the wand, I also like the wand as it is conical shaped with a fine pointed end which allows you to get right into the corner of the lashes to those very fine tiny lashes. I would have to say that this mascara is my favorite for the everyday woman who really needs that extra boost that extends the lashes without having to use false lashes as it is buildable, doesn't smudge, is tear proof and is also kind to the lashes with vitamins and waxes to encourage lash growth.
Paraben free, CODE VLM is not tested on animals

NATURAL PRODUCTS THAT ARE 'GREEN'

At LashInc head quarters we like to promote being green, so once again this issue I have sourced two separate products that are both very holistic and are environmentally friendly and certified 100% natural.

Hydrating face masque: Price £13.95 & Skin Food moisture cream Price £9.95 for 75ml, £6.95 for 30ml, or £2.25 for 10ml, from John Bell & Croydon, call 0115 9448200 or visit **www.weleda.co.uk**

WELEDA IRIS HYDRATING MASQUE

contains iris root extract and cucumber extract to help the skin to retain its optimal moisture level while also cooling and soothing the skin. High quality almond oil and jojoba oil soften and strengthen the skin's own protective barrier so that the skin is better able to withstand future dehydration. I suffer from very dry skin and I found this mask amazing for that winter skin that looks battered from daily stresses, poor diet and pollution, it really brightened and smoothed the skin that left it feeling softer to the touch. Once you have applied the masque it is best left on for a good ten minutes and mostly your skin will pull it in to the skin leaving little residue on the surface, it is like a drink for the skin.

WELEDA SKIN FOOD

has been a cult favourite since 1962 it is ideal for rough dry skin or thirsty skin that needs replenishment. It is used by makeup artists on the fashion circuit for its ability to bring back lacklustre skin to life, miraculously improving the skins appearance, it is often used as a primer before makeup application as the natural plant oils and waxes within the formula provide a perfect base for powder application. The product contains Chamomile and Wild Pansy to sooth the skin, plus Rosemary to revitalise the skin with fragrance of Sweet Orange. The unique selling points of the Weleda range is that they do not put any nasty chemicals into their products they are free from artificial preservatives and parabens.

ANTI-AGEING SKIN PROTECTOR SPF30 PRIMER *30ml*

has just won the 'Beauty Shortlist Awards 2014' as one of the best primer products on the market. The product has proven skincare benefits and offers a broad spectrum defence against UVA and UVB rays to prevent sun damage and premature ageing. I found that when using this product under makeup it allowed the makeup to be applied with ease and gave a really luminescent radiance to the skin, a great product for everyday use, however not a great product to use on your brides or for photographic makeup given that the product has SPF in the ingredients it did give a flash back to the face. It has now become a personal favourite though as I find my makeup does not budge when I am out and about and I love the fact that I am protected from harmful rays all year round.

Not tested on animals, free from Parabens, Lanolin, Mineral oil, SD alcohol, formaldehyde, SLS and artificial colours

Price £36.00, 30ml, available from www.shop.arkskincare.com, Head Office: 0208 339 6110, email **help@arkskincare.com**

INTRODUCING - THE LASHBUG!

LashBugs are a brand new innovative idea to allow lashers more comfort and ease whilst picking up lashes. These amazing little bugs sit comfortably on the back of your hand and can hold up to 6 strips at one time. They can be stored individually in their own boxes and be set aside for different clients who require different lengths, diameters and curvatures. They are a more hygienic way of placing lashes as the strips are not in contact with skin at any time and they are almost weightless. By placing the strips on the rounded LashBug you will find that the lashes fan out naturally so allows you to pick up perfect fans or individual lashes effortlessly. Also suitable for lashers who may have a reaction to strips on the skin.

They are made from colourful, soft foam, look great, feel great and will add lovely bright colour to your work area or station.
Also available are the Polymer LashBugs which are slightly smaller and more definitive.

The LashBugs are the creation of Eileen Frances and are available to purchase from **www.getbeautifullashes.com** amongst other distributors listed below in Eileen's story.

Eileen has kindly shared her story with us of how the LashBugs were born!

How was Lashbug conceived? The lash bug came about as many great inventions do, by the presence of necessity. I was taught in my first training course, to spill out loose lashes onto a sponge and set them all up on end by hand in order to grab them more easily. Well, I soon realized that using lashes sold on sticky tape strips and worn on the back of my hand during the application process was much easier, and this is the method of procedure that I became comfortable with. Until, the day when I realized that my skin was growing tired of two sided sticky tape.

Being that I am a fastidious person, I was always careful to return my strips of lash extensions to the proper box each time. Returning lashes to the proper box each time was important to me. The quick selections of a desired length, diameter and curl are important. Allowing lash strips to get all mixed up would waste lashes and time, and one might end up with an unexpected look on their client.

Returning lashes to proper boxes became a bit messy... curling ends etc. The worst problem was that once the tape was removed from the original backing, the stick would wear off. The next time I needed to use them, I would have to use a piece of two sided sticky tape on the back of my hand and place the twice used strip of lash extensions onto that. I grew weary of this. This was a constant irritant to my skin. I was also displeased with the back of my hand as a pallet, as it was not smooth or curved enough. However, lashing is difficult, anything to make it a bit easier was good...I needed to use the back of my hand, what other choice was there, spilling loose lashes out onto a sponge?

Then, last April I had the great fortune of having a master class with

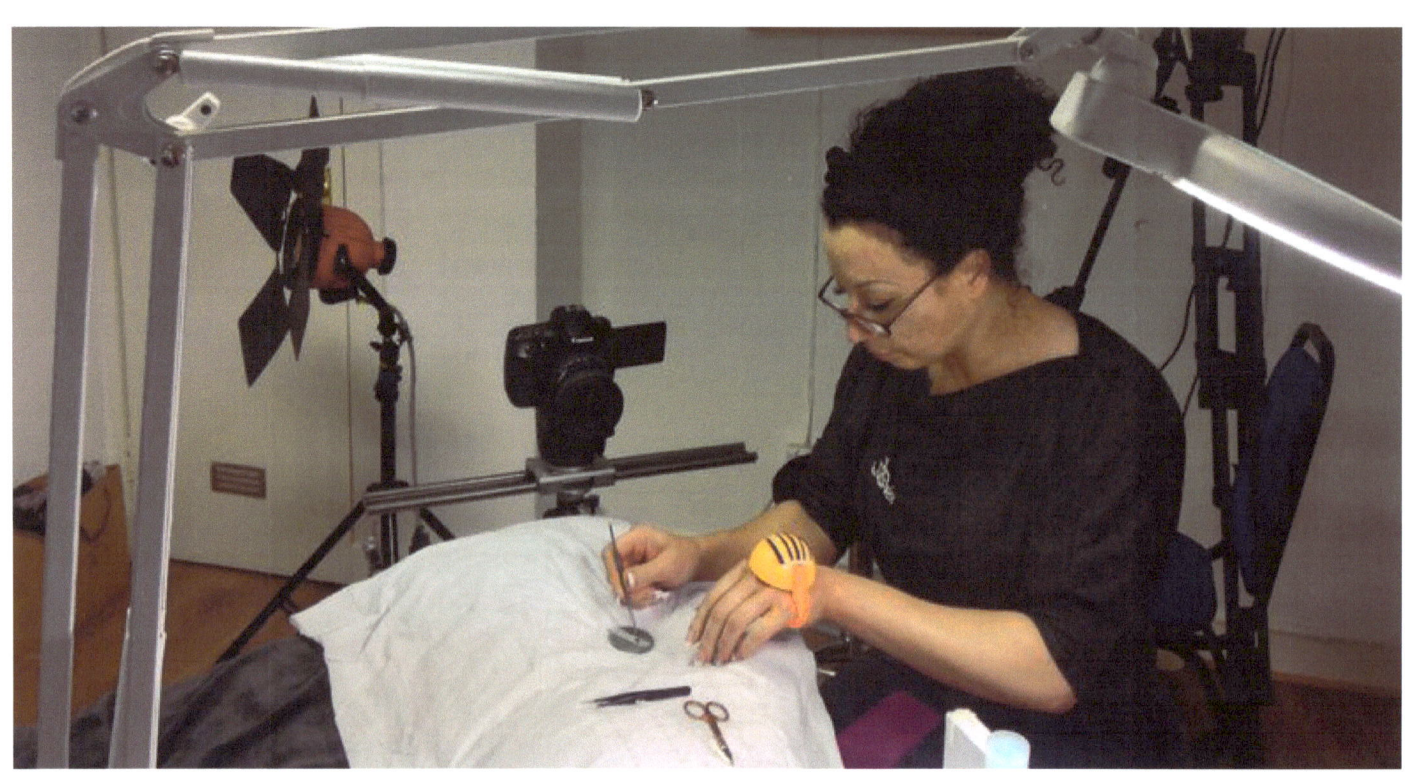

Teresa Smith. She was amazing, she taught me the secrets that would expand my lashing capabilities to a level I never knew existed. It was in Teresa's class that I learned there was another method of holding lashes, as she used a very nice tile lash pallet. My problem was I felt awkward using the tile method. I was already too accustomed to the back of my hand. Ergonomically I felt more comfortable with the flexibility of movement, using my hand. Reaching for my lashes from the tile coupled with learning to fan fine lashes ...I was lost.

One morning I woke up thinking about the shape of a dome, and how that might help with fanning. Upon further contemplation, I needed to solve the problem of how to attach one to the hand that would not interfere with comfort and movement. I needed a material that would be almost weightless. It had to be something light and unobtrusive. If I wanted to share with others, it needed to be adjustable or one size fits all.

Putting together a prototype was easy after my concept materialized in my mind. I knew what materials I wanted to use, having studied various options. I tested out the first bug, on May 8th 2014 and with minor adjustments that needed to be made it was complete, I was ready to share the brilliant idea, one that would spare me and many fellow lashers the problems I had set out to solve.

An unexpected side benefit to the LashBug is that I can store away multiple styles on various bugs. For example, my client who wears the B curl style from 11mm to 13mm has the pink bug, the D curl on the blue bug, etc., etc. As many combinations as you can imagine. As you see in one of my pictures, this can get out of control, especially, if you have access to as many bugs as you want, like I do!

We have two types of Lashbugs. The soft larger ones and the poly smaller ones. I love both, but the soft ones I favour most. It has been great fun marketing the LashBug. I could not have guessed the response. It has not been one year yet and now my LashBugs are hard at work all over the world. With distributors in New Jersey with Skynlash Studio, Seattle with Kim Monique and London Brows, and in the United Kingdom with Hanna Putjato, We have inquiries about distribution from Canada and Italy as well.

Thank you again Kim Gibb, for your kind offer to write an article on LashBugs.
Warmest Regards,
Eileen Frances
Beautiful Lashes and LashBugs

I'm sure everyone will agree that the LashBugs are the most amazing accessory for all you lashpreneurs out there and will soon be something you cannot live without.

Thank you to Eileen for sharing her story with us and also for the lovely colourful photos. I'm sure we will all want to purchase every colour and our client's will be very curious and amused to see all the lovely little LashBugs around salon's worldwide!

By Kim Gibb

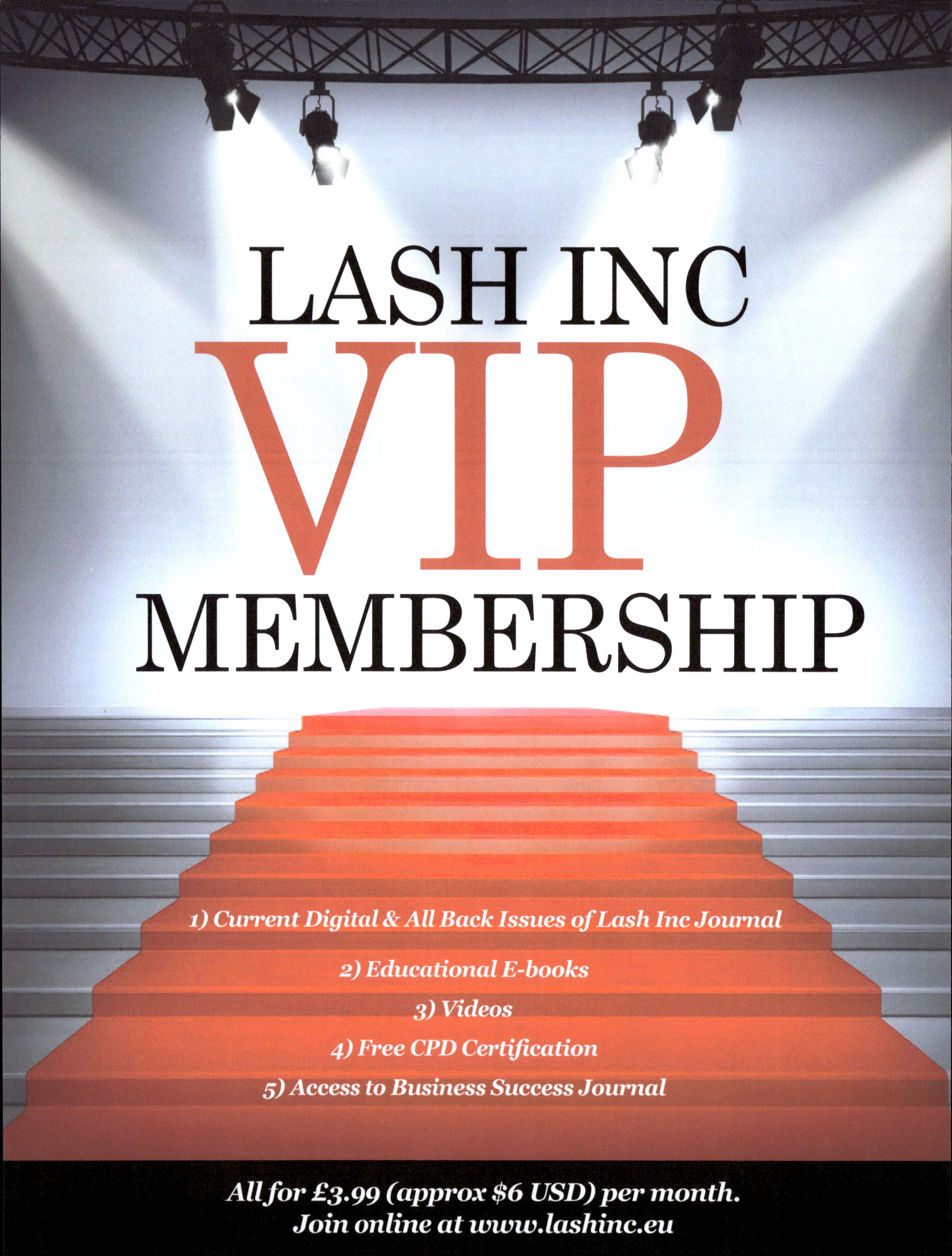

LASH INC
VIP
MEMBERSHIP

1) **Current Digital & All Back Issues of Lash Inc Journal**

2) **Educational E-books**

3) **Videos**

4) **Free CPD Certification**

5) **Access to Business Success Journal**

All for £3.99 (approx $6 USD) per month.
Join online at www.lashinc.eu

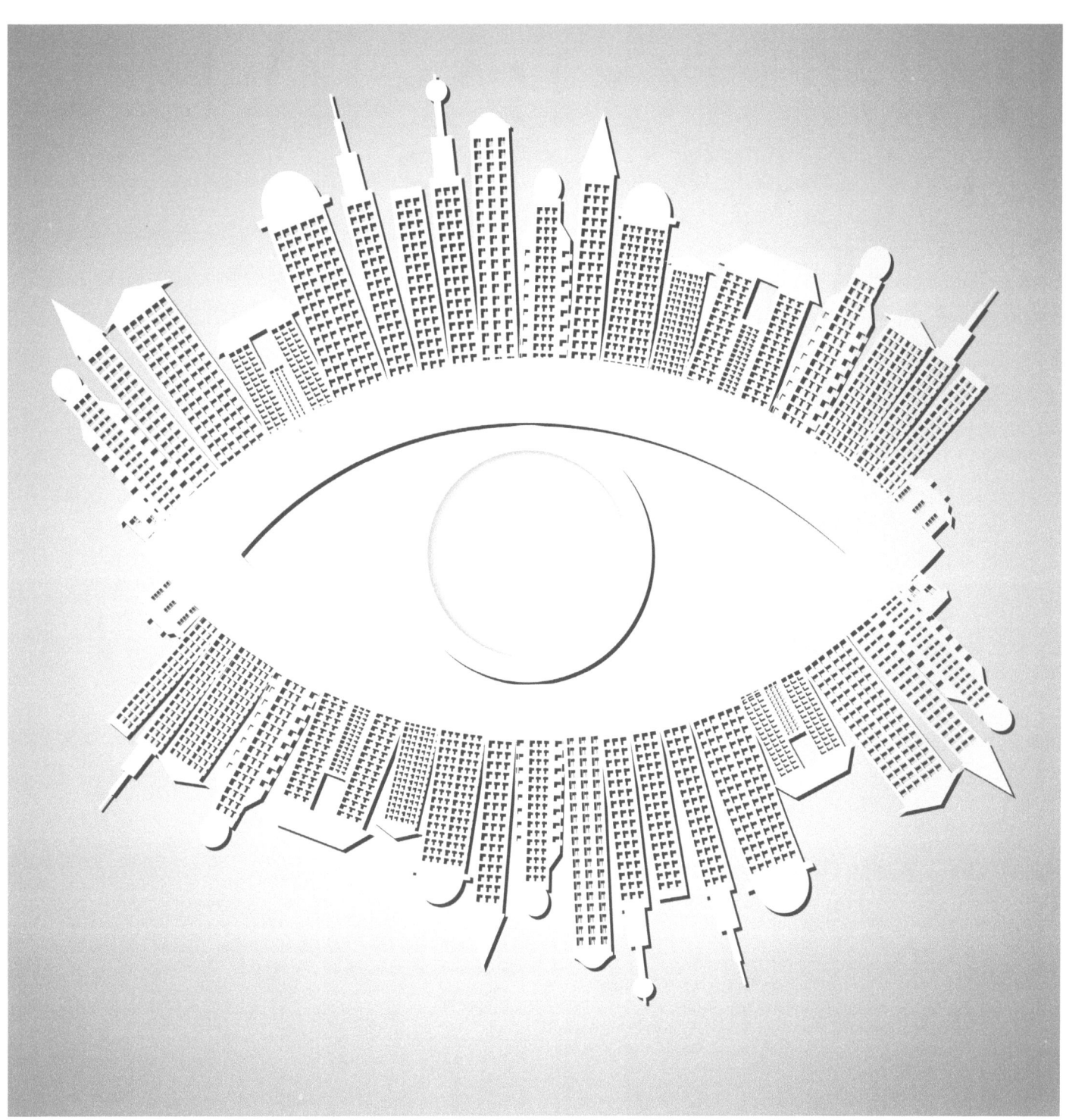

Business

BACK TO BASICS – CUSTOMER SERVICE

It's your first time getting eyelash extensions. You are nervous. You have researched licensed eyelash extension professionals in your area. You have narrowed it down to a couple locations.

Your first call is to Studio A. The voicemail instructs you to leave name and number to schedule an appointment. At Studio B there is a voicemail that states they will be calling you back with in 24 hours and or can book an appointment online.

You try to schedule online but you are not sure exactly what your scheduling for- Classic set? Volume? what does it all mean?

At the end of the day you receive a call back from Studio B. The eyelash extension professional educates you on what to expect prior to your arrival. You receive a formal email and are informed that you will also receive a reminder text message 72 hours and 24 hours prior to your appointment.

Studio A returns your call 2 days later, maybe or not at all, to find that you have already scheduled with another lash artist.

This scenario is what sets you apart from other lash artists. Customer service relates to the service provided to customers before, during and after a purchase.

Not only is education, licensing, and insurance important but customers service should be your top priority. If you wish to be successful, no matter how big or small your business is, excellent customer service needs be at the heart of your business model. It is important to provide good customer service to all types of customers, including potential, new and existing customers.

During your service and when a client arrives, greeting them to say hello and introducing yourself is the start of their customer service experience. Upon arrival it's also important for them to complete an intake form. If it's your clients first time meeting you. Talk them through the entire process, it is important to explain each step to make them feel comfortable on how your session with them will transpire. It's very awkward having a stranger touch or place anything around your eyes when they are closed. Ask them if they would like to use the restroom before you start their appointment and show them where it is located.

Why is customer service so important for you, your business and your customer?
• Increases customer loyalty
• Increases the amount of money each customer spends with your business by trusting your expertise
• Increases customer confidence if they return or decide to go somewhere else based on their experience
• Increases positive word-of-mouth (reputation)

What is does it mean to give excellent customer service?
• Treat your customers with respect
• Follow up on feedback through customer comments
• Professionalism: Skill, good judgment, and polite behavior is expected. You are a licensed professional
• Punctuality: Scheduling time is important to both you and your customer
• Return follow-up calls within 24 hours
• Take the time to speak to the customer by voice. Texting may be acceptable depending on situation
• Understanding your customers' needs and wants
• Taking pictures of your clients (if they approve) and posting to social media
• Going out of your way to help them find your location
• Making your customer feel that they are one of the most important people in your business
• Always send them a note or email thanking them. After all, they are choosing you for their service

By Nikki Hagen
Licensed Esthetician
Master Lash Artist

HOW TO ATTRACT CUSTOMERS AND GROW YOUR CLIENT BASE.

Francine Widdows

Over the years the beauty industry has been saturated with beauty therapists, this means that to attract those clients we need to set ourselves apart from the competition. It also seems that "everyone" these days is trying to undercut one another because they have to in order to attract clients in our over populated industry.

wants – what would you be looking for in a therapist or their work that would attract you to want to go to them? Once you have figured this out you then need to make sure that you sell all of this to our clients.

For example:

When searching for a therapist your potential client would like to know that you are

to know a little about you (we don't mean your hobbies and where you went on holiday last year) but your passion in the industry, why you do what you do, what you can offer that no one else can etc. This doesn't need to drag on but clients always like to know a little about their therapist before they visit. Most importantly clients must see your work because this will

So how do we attract those clients and keep them coming back to us? The first thing to think about is what our consumer/client

qualified and insured because there are a lot of "therapists" out there who are not, so make sure you state this. Your client would also like

sell you to your clients. If you fail to showcase your work then how does your client know what to expect? Not only will this attract clients but it was also allow you to meet their expectations - within reason. However make sure that your photographs are of good quality and attractive, poor photos will not sell you!

Now that we have all of this information we need to put it out there in the places where it can be seen by people who are looking for that treatment. It is well known that the internet is now the place to go when searching for most things and this includes beauty treatments so you need to be on there. A good webpage and Facebook page is paramount for any beauty therapists and you will gain a lot of business off this.

When it comes to a webpage you have many options available to you, you can make them yourself or you can hire web designers to do the work for you (however this can sometimes be expensive). When designing a webpage think carefully about how you want it to look and how it will reflect your business. Do you want your business to look classy and professional or do you want it to look fun and funky? If you decide that you want to attract the higher end clientele then think about the colours you would use, probably soft subtle and pastel colours with clean lines and a simple lay out. If you wanted to attract the younger clients then you may decide to go for a more colourful page, with more shapes and a little bit busier, so think about who you want to attract. With any webpage make sure that it is easy to navigate as there is nothing more frustrating than visiting a page and not being able to find what you are looking for. Moving on from this ensure that your webpage is responsive - so this means that it works on both a PC and a tablet device. Most people now view webpages on their devices so a responsive theme is paramount.

Have a gallery page on your webpage where clients can see all of your work. If you can, keep all of your photos the same size and easy to access and make sure these show case your best work only. Also ensure you have your prices clearly stated (as this is what most potential clients want to know)and having a lash menu that offers variety for your clients is a must.

Link your webpage to your Facebook Business page, so that clients can redirect to this and see your latest updates on your Facebook page. You should have a separate page for your business and keep it as this only - business. The great thing about Facebook is that it is free, so use this to your advantage.

Facebook can easily be updated at any time of the day with easy access via our phones etc. Keep your Facebook page active with daily updates, photos of your work, hints and tips, client offers etc. Try to get people to interact with your posts as this will make them more visible to viewers. Always upload a photo because Facebook recognises photos rather than plain text. Facebook is now such a busy site that it controls what posts people see – so just because you have posted it does not mean that Facebook will make this visible to others unless they interact and make the post popular. Facebook is a very good tool to advertise your business so we suggest you do some in depth research on how you can properly use Facebook to build your business.

Now that you have these two main advertising sites we can consider where else you can advertise. However from experience the following methods are not overly effective and we will explain why:

Leaflets drops – leaflets can be expensive to print, time consuming to post and the likely hood that you leaflet drop someone who is looking for that specific treatment is slim.

Local Magazines – these can be expensive to add an advert and unless you place an advert in week after week and people realise you are the "real deal" otherwise then most people will skip over it.

Pamper Parties/school evening pamper for Mummies – these types of ladies are usually very busy Mums so lack the time and disposable income to spend on beauty treatments. They enjoy a discount treatment at a pamper evening but it's unlikely they will ever book in for a full price treatment.

Giving to Charity – to give a voucher to Charity is always a great way to give something back so it's a lovely gift, but the voucher is likely to be won by someone that wouldn't usually have a treatment, or if they do they already go elsewhere. So do not expect repeat custom from this.

Sign writing your car – this can sound like a great way of advertising, however most people will see your car on the move and trying to read or scribble down a number when driving is impossible. Sign writing is also not cheap so it can be a wasted investment.

However one of the best ways to advertise your work is for people to see it in person. Firstly make yourself a walking advertisement by either wearing your own work or getting another therapist to work on your. Perform treatments to showcase your work on your friends and family – or people you know that come into contact with a lot of people. When these people see your beautiful work they will ask where it was done and then your walking model can whip out a business card that you gave them. This type of advertisement is one of the best forms out there and can gain you a big client base.

The one thing to remember is that gaining clients takes time. It takes trial and error to find what works for you to get clients through your door. Always set yourself apart from your competition by doing things a bit different as this will get you noticed. Continue to put yourself in the places where people are looking for what it is that you offer. Actually doing the treatment is only part of your business, attracting the clients now that's this hard bit – but continue to persist and they will come.

9 KEY AREAS OF A BUSINESS GROWTH EDUCATION (PART 1)

One of the big mistakes I've seen most business owners make over the years is to think that their current level of education will see them through the dynamic changing world of Business that we live in.

This is usually because they think that running a business is about the knowledge they have for being able to do the "job" of that business. Not true!

When they start to appreciate the real level of knowledge they are going to need, some Entrepreneurs head for the hills, while others pay the ultimate price for their lack of a broad Business education and fail or go bust. A few smart Business Owners seek out Coaching, Mentoring and Support to bridge the gap from where they are to where they want to be.

Shockingly, 80% of Start Up's don't make it to the 5 year point! Now imagine if somebody told you those were the odds before you got on a plane – would you fly? I bet if you are honest you wouldn't!

When I first got involved in personal development and reaslised that if I wanted to Earn more I needed to Learn more - the impact was almost immediate and I saw my sales increase.

Some Professions like Accountants and Lawyers force their members to complete a minimum number of Continuing Personal Development (CPD) hours to remain current and up to speed on changes to the Law etc. Just think about the financial success these professions enjoy, it's no accident.

The crazy thing is that as Business Owners nobody forces us to keep learning new skills.

When I started Business Coaching & my F10 Mastermind over 11 years ago, I wanted to create an environment for growth that is based in a Balanced Business Growth Education.

What do I mean by this?

I mean being able to understand ALL the critical functions within your business, not just Sales & Marketing for example. After all if you sell your product or service and never get paid it's a waste of time!

So lets take a look at the 9 Strategic and Tactical Business Growth Drivers I Coach my clients in so they build and grow a business that generates wealth for them.

As we go through these together I suggest, as your coach, that you assess how good your skills and knowledge level is for each area with 1 being very poor, 10 excellent.

This way you'll be benchmarking your current skill levels and get a perspective on where you need to invest time learning to grow your business moving forward.

After all if you are not growing you are dying. Lets start with:

1 - MINDSET:

The day to day reality of running and growing a business is that it's tough and you'll face failure, rejection, setbacks and adversity. How you choose to respond to these will ultimately have more of an impact on your success than you can ever realise.

In my experience 80% of your success is based in your mental skills, resilience, positivity, belief, confidence, focus and creativity to name a few.
As the saying goes..."the man who says he can and the man who says he can't are both usually right".

Growth Tip: Set up the success habits of reading a business book for a min of 20 minutes every day and turn dead time or down time, like driving, working out or walking the dog into growth time by listening to Podcasts, Online Programs and Motivations CD's. This is the fuel that will help you go the distance.
A word of caution though, even the most positive can do mindset will not beat an outdated business model. Your mindset is critical but finding the right market is vital.

2 - VISION:

We start with the big picture first. Where do you want your business to be in the next 3/5 years? What Sales and Profits will you be making? What countries will you be operating in? What markets will you be serving? How many people will be working for you? Do you want to sell the business for Asset Wealth or build it for a Lucrative Lifestyle?
These questions are critical, as without a destination we just end up going round in circles. Think about it, would you get into a car to go on holiday with no idea of the destination?

It's important to find your bigger Vision, or what is sometimes referred to as your "Why" power. The reason you are doing what you do is more than just about money. It's about making somebody elses life better, by helping them solve a problem or making their life or businesses easier, faster and less stressful....big drivers in today's world.

Growth Tip: Take 15 min a day to review your vision. This can be powerful if you can put it on Keynote slides or Power Point and mix with Music to get your emotions involved. Visit MindMovies.com who has some powerful software that also does this.

If you can see it in your mind you can hold it in your hand, so take time to work on the pulling power of your Vision. After all if your "WHY" is big enough you'll always find a way to win!

3 - STRATEGY:

Now we know your destination, we can start to evaluate and Plan HOW we pull it off. It amazes me how many of my clients over the years have called me to help them without a great vision, no documented plan to navigate by.

Do you have one right now that you to look at on your wall every day? If not start planning! Your strategy should have evaluated the true market opportunity not what you just feel is a good market. As I say to a lot of clients "act on fact" and the numbers need to stack up.

Start by answering these Strategy Questions:
Where is the Niche with the biggest pain or problem? (Profit will follow)
Describe who they are in detail? Imagine they are standing in front of you now.
How much disposable income do they have to solve their problem? How high is the level of desire to fix the problem? (No desire means that making sales will be tough)
Can you get your product / solution in front of them for a low enough cost to make acquiring customers cost effective?
How can you test your market assumptions in a low cost low risk way? (Research is great – reality is better)

Growth Tip: Defining your growth strategy is never easy on your own so consider bringing in expert help. I offer a Strategic Planning Program and if you want to know more and claim your 3 FREE Training Videos on this key growth area visit PaulAvins.com

Remember thought, hope is not a strategy!!

4 - MARKETING:

OK, this is one of my personal favorites to study, and as a business owner your ability to generate leads into your business is one of the key success skills you'll need to learn and master.

This is a huge area and you have more and more ways to reach your customers so for now lets give you some of the fundamentals of marketing mixed with some practical and tactical tools you can use.

Lets start with the 3 M's of Marketing Mastery as I like to call them...

1. **Market** – your "who" of who you want to sell to.
2. **Message** – your "what" you are going to say to your target market that will connect to this challenges, problems and pains so that they see you as the solution provider to go to.
3. **Media** – your "how" of getting your message to your key target market so that they see it and most importantly respond to it.

Now what most business owners do in my experience is to spend more time on the "how" question for example, Social Media, Google Adwords, Facebook, Networking, direct mail, YouTube or whatever else newest "silver bullet" marketing platform being sold by online marketers.

I suggest clients invest time in learning skills like Copywriting that apply to all media, online and offline, you'll find you get great response if you have identified the right market.

As a business owner 80% of your time needs to be invested in the demand side of the business generating leads and future clients so you must get out of operations as fast as possible.

Growth Tip: Marketing is more about Math's than it is about creativity so make sure you know your numbers. To start with Cost per Lead, Cost per Sale and Lifetime Value then you test and measure differing creative.

People always get revved up when they realise just how much there is to learn on this subject that can be applied to their business.

To help you get started I have a Free Online Marketing Course 7 Sins of Marketing packed with advice on what NOT to do in your marketing that could be costing your Millions!! Grab your copy today at PaulAvins.com/7sinsofmarketing

In the next issue I'll be revealing the final 5 areas you need to understand and learn to master as a business owner if you want sustainable growth.

About Paul:

Paul Avins is an Award Winning Business Growth Coach, creator of the F10 Mastermind and a Business Speaker who has trained thousands of Entrepreneurs, Sales People and Teams all over the World. His passion to help business owners achieve personal and financial freedom from their business has led him to write a number of books including – 'Business SOS' and 'Business Truths' as well as creating many products, online training programs and tools to Accelerate Profitable Growth.

Artistically Created Lash Extensions

It's Not Just A Skill It's An ART

ArtisticLash.com
Michell@ArtisticLash.com

Advance Styling to Create Custom Sets of Lash Extensions

All Classes are Two Days and Offered Globally
Beginner and Advance Training
Product Knowledge | Business and Marketing Skills
Eye Anatomy | Sanitation | Eye Health
Adhesive Control | Taping Lower Lashes | Lash Layering
Full Sets vs Touch ups | Bottom Lash Application

Premium Quality Lash Products and Advance Lash Artistry Training

Lash Inc
Accreditation

The following training academies and individuals are accredited by Lash Inc.
Their training courses and qualifications meet all requirements for approval by our organisation.

United Kingdom & Ireland
Accredited Training Providers.

ENGLAND:

Love My Lashes
Sue Winter
7 Bremen Grove, Shenley Brook End,
Milton Keynes
MK5 7FJ
mklashes@gmail.com

Flirties
Unit 2, Tarlair Business Park
Tarlair Way,
Macduff
AB44 1RU
www.flirties.co.uk
0845 022 22 33

**East Anglian Beauty
Training**
maureen@eabt.co.uk
www.eabt.co.uk

**Sugarlash Academy
of Lash Artistry**
Vicky Rugg
www.sugarlashpro.com
info@sweetsugarlashes.com

SCOTLAND:

**Caledonian Therapy
Academy**
7 Newton Place
Glasgow
G3 7PR
www.ctacademy.co.uk
Tel: 01423329251

Flirties
Unit 2, Tarlair Business Park
Tarlair Way,
Macduff
AB44 1RU
www.flirties.co.uk
0845 022 22 33

Francesca Middleton
LASHacademy Training & Products
Contact: rachel@lashbyfrancesca.co.uk
Web: www.lashbyfrancesca.co.uk

IRELAND:

Monika Wojtysiak
DeviLash Lash extensions Atelier &
Training Centre.
16/1 8 William Street Galway
Ireland
devilashireland@gmail.com

United States Of America
Accredited Training Providers.

Benita Lash Studio
18321 W. Lake Houston Pkwy
Suite 305
Humble,
TX 77346
benitaramos@outlook.com

Amy Young
Love Those Lashes LLC
http://nomascara.com
http://lovethoselashes.blogspot.com
Tel: 513.280.6550

Lucy Argent
LA Lash Academy
137 Bay Street #8, Santa Monica, CA
90405, United States
Phone:+1 424-200-8278

Lash Inc
Accreditation

TRAINING DIRECTORY

UK and Ireland

LASHacademy Training & Products

Contact: rachel@lashbyfrancesca.co.uk
Web: www.lashbyfrancesca.co.uk

Products

The LASHacademy supply products that are of the highest quality and most affordable to professional lash technicians. We ship worldwide.

Training Dates: Ongoing

Frankie Widdows

Contact:
eyelash.extension.kent@gmail.com
07714 638405

Web:
www.eyelashextensiontraining.co.uk

Master lash artist Frankie Widdows is head trainer at the Institute of Eyelash Excellence. She provides outstanding training from foundation level through to advanced lash techniques and Russian volume eyelash extensions. She also provides continued online support and tutorials as well as 24/7 access to her for the rest of your lash career.

Training Dates: Ongoing

Ireland

Ms Diva
Training Cork & Dublin
Web: http://www.msdiva.ie/
Contact: Aoife@msdiva.ie
0870 991 991

Michelle Ryan

Michelle@flirties.co.uk
07825924920
www.flirties.co.uk
www.stalhambeauty.co.uk

Michelle Ryan is an experienced and passionate lash technician who has a wealth of knowledge that she loves to share with her students. As a trainer for Flirties, she constantly strives to improve the standard of eyelash extensions across the board. Being a busy therapist herself gives Michelle the ability to support students not just with training but to also offer help and advice in other areas of setting up and running a business.

USA

Sinful Lashes
Luxury Products and Quality Training.
Tel-1-818-970-7151
Email-Sinfullashes@gmail.com
www.sinfullashes.com

-Luxury products at competitive prices. Featuring our Red Ruby Volume Adhesive.
-Quality, in-depth training located in Los Angeles. We also travel the US bringing our Classic and Volume training to you.

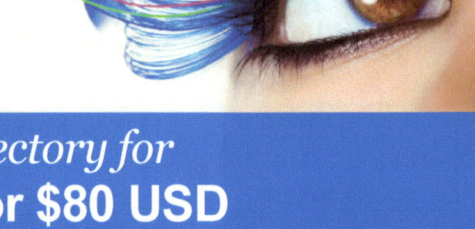

68

SUPPLIER DIRECTORY

USA & Canada

SkynLash Academy
Training Courses
Continuing Education at it's Finest

Skype Training Available
Basic Lashes to Advanced Volume
Lashcoat & Lashbrow Training
SkynLash Shop for the Finest Lash Supplies
www.skinlashstudio.com
info@skinlashstudio.com
732-618-2096 NJ USA

Novalash
http://www.novalash.com/
contact@novalash.com
1-866-430-1261

RevitaLash® Cosmetics
cservice@revitalash.com
www.revitalash.com

Angel Eyelashes
Eyelash Supplier to
Professionals

www.angeleyelashes.com
info@angeleyelashes.com

Aesthetic Image is the professional's source for innovative and luxury lash products. We offer the highest quality lashes, adhesives, and cutting edge lash tools. Our exclusive Pro Lash System provides lash artists with a faster and more efficient way to lash. We ship worldwide. Shop 24/7 online at ailashes.com
info@ailashes.com / ailashes.com

Sugar Lash
Eyelash extension & training provider

www.sweetsugarlashes.com
www.facebook.com/sugarlashPRO

Sweet Lash
www.sweetlash.com
info@sweetlash.com
377 Marshall Way N #1
Layton, UT 84041

Lash Affair by J.Paris
www.LashAffair.com
info@lashaffair.com
1.800.608.2420
We sell Luxury Lash Extension Products
& Global Certifications
We ship and train globally as well.

Sinful Lashes
Luxury Products and Quality Training.

Tel-1-818-970-7151
Email-Sinfullashes@gmail.com
www.sinfullashes.com

-Luxury products at competitive prices.
Featuring our Red Ruby Volume Adhesive.
-Quality, in-depth training located in Los
Angeles. We also travel the US bringing our
Classic and Volume training to you.

Flirties
BeautyTrix
Tel. 0845 022 2233
www.beautytrix.me

Lash Perfect
0208 500 9028
info@lashperfect.co.uk
www.lashperfect.co.uk

- Professional and accredited training available from expert trainers at competitive prices throughout the UK
- Internationally renowned and available worldwide through over 25 overseas distributors

UK / Europe
Novalash
http://www.novalash.com/uk/
CONTACT@NOVALASH.COM
+44(0)1273 862399

elite lash

UK/Ireland
http://www.elitelash.co.uk/
Elite Lash Academy
Mall Road
Monaghan
Ireland
Tel: +3534772580
+353868593699
Email: santa.jodka@gmail.com

NOUVEAU BEAUTY GROUP

Nouveau Lash
Nouveau Beauty Group
http://www.nouveaubeautygroup.com/

Tel: 0844 8016820

VZ Hair and Glamour Ltd
International Distributor - Affordable Beauty Supplies
T: +44 (0)755 492 5551
E: info@vzhairandglamour.com
W: www.vzhairandglamour.com

• Professional LashBlack 3 Week Semi Permanent Mascara: Made in England & EU Certified
• Eyelash Extension Medical Grade Glues made in England – Ultra Diamond Pro:
fast drying - Senses for Sensitive eyes: low vapour odour, perfect for trainers and beginners
• Individual Mink Eyelashes 100% Real Siberian Handmade Lashes

My Beautiful Eyes
Mylash, Myscara, Mybrows
http://www.mybeautifuleyes.eu/
sales@beautyinnovator.co.uk

LASHacademy Training & Products
Contact: rachel@lashbyfrancesca.co.uk
Web: www.lashbyfrancesca.co.uk

Products
The LASHacademy supply products that are of the highest quality and most affordable to professional lash technicians. We ship worldwide.